EMPOWERED BY THE STORM

Releasing The Past And Embracing The Light

JILL RIPLEY

Copyright © 2025 Jill Ripley

All rights reserved. No part of this book may be reproduced, stored, or transmitted by any means—whether auditory, graphic, mechanical, or electronic—without written permission of both publisher and author, except in the case of brief excerpts used in critical articles and reviews. Unauthorized reproduction of any part of this work is illegal and is punishable by law.

Contents

Dedication v
Introduction vii

Chapter 1:   Sobriety 1
Chapter 2:   Learning to Love Yourself 6
Chapter 3:   Ego 15
Chapter 4:   Consciousness 20
Chapter 5:   Feelings 30
Chapter 6:   Fuel for the Body and Soul 38
Chapter 7:   Masks 41
Chapter 8:   Spiritual Awakening 46
Chapter 9:   Enlightenment 50
Chapter 10: Love 52
Chapter 11: Physical Reality 55
Chapter 12: Programming 61
Chapter 13: Words 66
Chapter 14: Self-Deprecation 69
Chapter 15: Grace 74
Chapter 16: Fear 77
Chapter 17: Worry 81
Chapter 18: Grief 83

Chapter 19: The Words You Use in Life Matter ... 88
Chapter 20: The Inner Child(ren) 92
Chapter 21: Masculine and Feminine Energies 94
Chapter 22: The Law of Attraction 97
Chapter 23: Practice Being Less Reactive 99
Chapter 24: Helpful Practices 101

Conclusion 119

Dedication

First, I want to dedicate this book to my greatest teachers, my children Joe, Jamie, and Jenna. Each one of my children is very special to me, and they have all taught me something unique and different. The very nature of parenting means that we set ourselves aside for the sake of caring for another. This in itself is a great lesson and a great gift. Aside from this, each child has such a different personality and propensity for trying different things (good and bad) that we cannot help but learn from them. I am truly blessed.

Next, I would like to thank each and every human guide that has given me life experience. Again, good and bad. From the people who aided me in life, I learned compassion and grace. I learned how it feels to be supported and loved. Many of the people who supported me in life were not related and had no stake in the outcome of my life. They only had a desire within themselves to help another. For this I am truly thankful for the lesson of compassion.

To the people in my life who hurt me, whether intentionally or unintentionally, I also say thank you for the lessons I learned in strength, perseverance, and growth. At this point in my life, I feel well seasoned. Kind of like sweet and salty chocolate—the salt enhances the sweetness. I am grateful for ALL the challenging experiences, as I have learned the gift of forgiveness. There is no feeling more freeing than that of forgiving someone who wounded you, whether or not they ever apologized for their actions, or understood that they hurt you, or even cared. Emotionally, physically, or spiritually. It is all part of the journey of becoming.

Introduction

The ideas and stories and revelations in this book are a compilation of my life experiences and how I believe they play out and this is my reality. You may or may not resonate with the ideas as I believe them to be, and if that is the case, that is totally fine. We all live life according to our interpretation of our individual experiences. It is important for you to find your own way of understanding and believing in moving forward in life. But, if it does resonate with you and it makes sense to you then I am grateful to be able to share my experiences and to be able to give you a unique perspective on things.

All of the ideas in this book are my own understanding of the lessons I have learned from life's teachers throughout my life's experiences, as well as the concepts delivered to me in deep meditations.

Because of all those life lessons that I have been through, I have come to know and learn and change in so many different and wonderful ways. I think one of the greatest lessons I have learned is being open to being wrong, or seeing things from a new perspective.

Empowered by the Storm

I look at things from my past and I see where I could have been closed minded and where I could have done things differently. Not that I am lamenting, or sorry that things turned out the way that they did. It is all part of the journey and part of who we are. However, if I can contemplate without judgment, it can help me to make choices in the future that would be more in alignment with my dharma or true nature.

So, who am I and why on God's green earth would you bother reading a book written by me??? I ask myself the same question. But wait, don't run away. I have an answer for that. While I am not famous, I haven't made tons of money in business, and I have never gone on a mountainous retreat to Bali or some other fantastic destination, I can tell you I have experienced a ton of life's shitstorms. Along with life's shitstorms comes a whole lot of maneuvering, problem solving and growth. That is, if you are one of the people who allow yourself to grow from these experiences. I can tell you that from all of the storms I have been through, I have grown to be a person who has learned to be more open, compassionate and loving toward myself and others.

I have experienced abandonment from my mother at the age of two, the death of my father at age three, the loss of one of my brothers at age four, the loss of the grandmother who raised me at age fourteen. I have been through physical and emotional abuse, sexual molestation, and the instability of moving through the foster care system. I became

Introduction

pregnant at the age of sixteen and had to navigate the experience of having a new baby at seventeen, while still being somewhat of a baby myself. I can tell you that being a single mom on public assistance at that age really didn't do much for my self-esteem either, however, I was blessed with the most amazing and wonderful son a mother could ask for.

At the age of twenty-one I met an amazing man that I fell deeply in love with. We had so much in common, and we had so much fun together, I couldn't believe how fortunate I felt. I married the love of my life at age twenty-eight and I thought this amazing relationship was the reward for having endured such a rough beginning. Not only was he handsome, kind, thoughtful and good to me, but he was an amazing father to my son. I felt like I finally had the amazing life I had always longed for.

Shortly after we married, we decided to add to our beautiful family and had two amazing daughters together, but even this blessing was wrought with hardship. I suffered postpartum depression with our first daughter and subsequently, prenatal and postpartum depression with our second. It took me several years, medication and counseling to somewhat recover from this.

Just after our youngest daughter was born, my husband had an accident that totaled the truck that he used for his primary business and was out of work for nine months. The accident was not his fault, but because the other driver was in a rental vehicle, collecting from the insurance was near impossible. We ended up having to settle for $15,000 on a truck that we had to spend $120,000 to replace. We had to take a home equity line of credit for him just to be able to return to generating income. This was a huge emotional and financial strain.

My husband was a workaholic, and having his sense of identity stripped from him so abruptly, caused him an immense amount of anxiety and depression. He was miserable, and I was unsure how to best help him. At the time, I suggested to him medication and therapy. He agreed he needed help. He opted for medication but never opened up to the idea of therapy. I think this was a huge mistake. I don't feel he ever truly recovered from this experience.

Eventually, he was able to replace his truck and resume full operation of his business, but things were never really the same after that.

Once my husband returned to the daily grind, the business just seemed to take over. He spent long hours working and time after work at the pub trying to release the stress of the day before returning home.

Being a stay-at-home mom, I felt overwhelmed satisfying all the duties of parenthood and home making without the support of my partner. Not only did the full responsibility of the children and household chores fall on me, but I was also responsible for all the yard work and most of the home maintenance. With my husband spending so much time away from home, I felt as though I had no one to talk to, no one to rely on.

Introduction

The growing demands of my husband's business on him, and my deepening sense of overwhelm caused us both to increase our dependence on alcohol.

I had expressed to my husband that I had a severe drinking problem and I would like for us to quit drinking together. At that time, he was unable to support me in this request. I knew that without his support in quitting, I would be unable to be successful in giving up alcohol. This put a huge strain on our marriage, and in 2013, after twenty years together and fourteen years of marriage, I found myself divorced, heartbroken, and alone.

It hasn't always been easy for me to love myself, and I continue to have instances where I forget my worth. I have gone through my fair share of self-loathing, depression, self-abuse, and medicating with alcohol. It is only after many years of reflection and self-education that I now find myself ready to share what I have learned and how it has helped me. When contemplating the value I may or may not provide in writing this book, I came across the Mindvalley podcast episode "How to Write a Book in 8 Days" with Neeta Bhushan. The thing that she said that prompted me to act was that, when questioning why anyone would want to read a book by me, is to understand that what I have to say has never before been written from MY perspective and there are people in the world who NEED to hear it from ME. Wow, I had never really thought of it that way. I do indeed have a unique perspective on things and have spent countless hours listening to a myriad of self-help teachers, read dozens upon dozens of personal development books, read tons of blogs and spent numerous hours soul searching. It would stand to reason that I may have something to offer, and if you have ever thought of writing a book, just know that the same goes for you. We all have a unique perspective and there are others out there that will resonate with it and can benefit from your work. Now, I can tell you it has taken me a lot more than eight days to write this work. There are times when I forget that my experiences have value and I put the work aside for a while. I am always drawn though at some point to come back to this work. My higher guidance tells me when to get crackin' and get on the stick. Sometimes I listen, and sometimes I let life get in the way. I don't beat myself up over this though. I am trusting in divine guidance and the inner knowing that the information will come out when it is meant to.

I want to share my personal perspective with you in the hopes that I can relate what I have learned in a way that resonates with you and has a positive impact on your life.

We are all here to be teachers for each other and we are all here to learn from each other. Your children come through you, and you are their guide and their teacher, but they in turn are your teacher as well. Being a parent is hard work and each challenge you face with your children shapes and molds the way you experience life. The rewards for parenting are immeasurable. I have learned so much from my

Introduction

children, and I am looking forward to my grandchildren teaching my children.

There isn't a person alive who doesn't have struggles in their daily existence. Some people have the ability to work through these challenges, while other people succumb to a victim mentality. What I hope to instill in you is that even though you may have had a tendency to live in the victim mentality in the past, it is not your destiny to remain there. As long as we are breathing, we have the opportunity to choose a new path and to adopt a new belief or belief system.

No matter who has hurt you, no matter what has happened to you, no matter what you have done, you have the ability to rise above it and live the amazing life you were meant to experience. Until your very last earthly breath, you have the capability of choosing a new mindset. You can forgive yourself and others for any and **ALL** transgressions, whether real or perceived. There is nothing in life that is unforgivable. It may seem that there is, but I am here to tell you otherwise. You will understand more as we go on.

Chapter 1

Sobriety

It was evident to me at this time that if I were ever to be able to heal and grow, I would need to get sober. This is something I had tried numerous times to accomplish but had failed at over and over again.

Alcohol was my very best friend for a huge portion of my life. From age eleven to age forty-seven, I was never truly fully present, nor could I really experience and work through the many challenges life had to offer me. I would use alcohol to numb the pain of trauma over and over and over. It became part of who I thought I was. For most of my life, I really hadn't considered it was too much of a problem. I thought that because I always functioned competently and did all the things required of me, that it was just a part of life. Very often I barreled through life nursing a hangover, but making sure to complete everything on my plate.

I would get up early every day, and work out, even if I had only had a few hours of sleep due to the alcohol waking me up. I would put a happy face on for the world, even when I had to go to work. I did all that was required of me. I think it's harder to face the fact that you have a real problem, when you are not lying in a gutter.

It would take me two years after the divorce from my husband for me to finally get sober.

My last drink was March 8, 2015. It is my belief that if you are truly alcohol dependent, it takes a strong reason WHY to overcome the urge to drink. I had a reason to believe one of my kids was at risk of self-harm and I desperately wanted to be alert and aware, if I was needed, in the event of an emergency. It was in that moment of crisis and awareness of the potential harm to one of my children that I finally mustered up the courage to say ENOUGH.

I was also guided by an angel in human form who relayed their own personal story of alcohol abuse and their method of self-accountability that gave me the hope that this time, I would finally succeed.

I was scheduled to meet an old friend of my former-mother-in law's for lunch. She was a great help to me in caring for her in her later years when she developed dementia and I wanted to thank her by taking her out to lunch. I really didn't want to make it to lunch that day, as I was extremely hung over. I had been so distraught by the idea that one of my children was at risk for self harm that I used copious amounts of alcohol to numb the hurt. But, I didn't

Sobriety

want to disappoint her, so I made myself go. It was the best decision I have ever made.

When I showed up to the restaurant, she took one look at me and said "You don't look so good." I told her "I don't feel so good!" I sheepishly admitted to her the details of the situation and my ongoing battle with alcohol. I had wanted to quit drinking for so many years, but I felt alcohol had such a hold on me, but I was terrified that one of my kids would need me and I would be too drunk to help.

She opened up to me about her own past struggles with alcohol and from the sounds of it, she had been drinking a lot more than I (which I did not think was possible) and she told me about the day she got sober, what worked for her and how it may be able to help me. I was just so desperate, I would be open to just about anything.

She told me how she had done something she felt was so shameful and that was enough for her to realize alcohol was the ruin of her life. She decided to get a pocket calendar and mark and X on each day she did not drink. It was the physical sight of the X on the calendar each day that gave her the resolve to keep going. At the time of our lunch, she told me she had twenty-plus years of calendars with X's in her closet as a reminder of her sobriety, and continues daily to place the X.

Something about this simple task sounded so doable for me, I decided to give it a try. On the way home, I bought a pocket calendar. The next day I began. For three months, I placed my X in the calendar and each day, I felt more and more determined that alcohol would no longer rule or ruin my life. After three months, I just knew I was done. That was in 2015.

I would like to say all my problems went away when I quit drinking, but that is not the case. Life will always have problems and circumstances that cause us pain, challenge our resolve and present us situations we need to overcome. But what I will say is that going through all these hardships sober, has allowed me to fully feel and heal through each experience.

I found myself having to reinvent myself once again. I finally thought I had a grip on things when the unimaginable happened. My youngest daughter and my former husband died tragically together in a motorcycle accident. Needless to say, this was by far the most challenging experience I had ever had to face.

I truly believe that had I not been sober through the process of grieving my daughter's passing, I would have drowned in a sea of despair. Being sober allowed me to feel all the emotions that came along with such a traumatic experience. Not that I enjoyed the feelings. It was so painful, there are truly no words to describe the anguish of a mother's heart torn to shreds at the loss of a beautiful soul that had been so deeply woven into the fabric of my existence. Had I succumbed to the invitation of temporary numbing relief of alcohol, I would not have had the wherewithal to move adequately through the grieving process. Had I not been sober, I am sure I would have

Sobriety

been unable to work through my grief with any semblance of compassion and grace.

Any type of substance dependence is merely a temporary numbing of a situation, and not actually a relief at all. Whether it be alcohol, drugs, food, pornography, social media or anything else that distracts your attention and numbs your feelings, these temptations are false friends. Offering you a temporary cover up of a situation that ultimately warrants and truly requires your unimpeded focus.

Life is a challenge, and while it may seem harmless to escape, you really can't move forward in life unless you fully experience the hurts and hurdles that arise. These distractions only serve to impede your progress on the hero's journey.

I tell you all this not to have you feel sorry for me, or to sound like I am lamenting my history. In fact, I often tell people that I have had the benefit of a hard life. I mean this sincerely. Would I have chosen any of this for myself? Absolutely not!!! But what I can tell you is that each and every experience has taught me something, and I have allowed myself to become stronger, more compassionate and more resourceful as a result.

Chapter 2

Learning to Love Yourself

There is not a person alive now, a person who has lived in the past, or a person who will ever live in the future, that does not have a story. It is up to each individual to make the choices that determine how their story will play out. Some people are given more dramatic circumstances that they have to overcome, but it is their choice whether or not they experience it in a healthy way, or if they succumb to the pressures and circumstances.

We live in an ocean; our bodies are our boat. We can either set the sails and have a direction or float along on the ocean our entire lives letting the waves and conditions of the water determine our course and our fate. Either way, we will go along the journey. If we are more deliberate in how we set our sails, the journey will be much smoother. Your success will directly correlate and correspond to your willingness to invest energy in your personal growth.

Learning to Love Yourself

One of the greatest keys to achieving this is to learn to love yourself, warts and all. You must accept that you have your flaws, but that you are also truly miraculous and amazing.

First thing you should understand is NO ONE owes you anything. Next thing, the only one you OWE anything to is YOURSELF. On the surface, this may sound like a selfish uncaring statement, but if you indulge me for a bit, you will understand where I am coming from.

When I was put on this earth, my mother gave me the gift of life. She did not owe me that gift. She certainly could have ended her pregnancy, but she chose to give me life. If she had stayed in my life, it would have been because she chose to be there and provide lifelong care for me, but she did not owe me that. If she did that, it would have been a gift to me. The gift she chose to give to me instead was to leave me and my brothers with my father and my grandmother. They chose to accept that role in my life. They could have just as easily declined. I was not owed their care and attention. I was blessed to have received it.

By the same token, I chose to give my children life, and I also chose to remain committed to raising them the best I could. This did not make me better than my mother. I just chose a different path. The paths we choose reflect the energy output of our soul. If you choose to put out positive energy, positive energy will return to you. Nothing is owed to you and you owe nothing. It is all a matter of what energy you choose to emanate and receive back in kind. This is Karma. Karma is the returning of energy output. You are a magnet for the energy you emit.

I have also come to realize; my children do not OWE me ANYTHING. If they chose to be involved in my life, I am grateful, but this is not a condition of my love for them. I gave them the gift of life and if given freely, without condition. It is up to them if they choose to continue to have a relationship with me. Of course, it is my hope that they do want to be involved with me and I would be deeply hurt if they chose otherwise, but I love them even if that were not the case. The same goes for friends and family. I have had many friends and family who have fallen in and out of my life for one reason or another, but if I am practicing unconditional love, I will still love them from a distance. I don't owe them my time or attention, and they do not owe me either. I love them no matter what.

When I say that the only one you owe anything to is yourself, I mean that you owe it to yourself to put out the type of energy you wish to have in your life. If you want to be loved, you must give love. If you want to be wealthy, you must be open to generosity. Mind you, generosity comes in many different forms and it goes both ways. You must be as open to receiving as you are to giving. Too many times in my life someone has offered to pay for lunch, or to give me something, and I would feel it necessary to decline. I would say "Oh, no, that is not necessary." or "Oh, no, I can't accept that." You must allow yourself to accept the gift and say a genuine "Thank you, that is so kind of you." People love to give. When you decline their offer to pay for lunch or dinner, or pass up a generous offer of something tangible, you ultimately deny that person the joy of giving you a gift. It is an ego construct that says "I am not worthy of this" or "What will this person think of me if I accept this gift?" They are not thinking anything ill of you if they are offering you something. They are emanating their true generous nature. And it is not just monetary. It can be the gift of a smile, time spent helping others, or even just taking time to listen to someone who needs support. If you want excitement in your life, you must look for things to get excited about.

You owe it to yourself to be kind, to be loving, to be generous, to embrace a positive outlook in life. When you suffer in despair, you suffer needlessly. I can't tell you how many countless hours I have spent ruminating negative scenarios over and over in my head, only to see later that the thing I worried about only served to drive me to a better path in life. It has become apparent to me that when I focus on the fact that things are always working out well for me, not only is my mind more at peace, but things actually seem to work out quicker.

The keys to your best life are love, compassion, and forgiveness. We will explore the deep need for you to love and forgive yourself and others, and to also have compassion for yourself and others.

If you are saying to yourself, "But she has no idea what happened to me, she has no idea how hard my life has been because of . . ." or "I could never forgive that person for . . . " or "I could never forgive myself for . . .," let me assure you that, even though my circumstances may not be the same as yours and I can never feel exactly as you have felt, I have had my fair share of things that I thought I could never forgive some people for, and some things I thought I could never forgive myself for. However, in order to have the life you have always wanted, this is exactly what you must do.

Now, one of the first things that must be understood is that forgiveness in no way suggests that what happened to you, or that thing you did was OK, or that you are letting someone or yourself off the hook. It simply means that you develop a deeper understanding of the divine nature of all people, including people who do harm to others.

When you embrace the understanding that people who hurt others do so because they have a deep hurt within themselves and are truly ignorant of healthy ways to release their pain, they project their pain outward to the easiest targets. If that person had competent coping skills, they would never have done harm to another.

So forgiveness is seeing that pain in another, and having compassion for the origin of that pain. It is being able to recall the hurt that was imposed upon you without feeling the anger well up inside YOU. For when the anger is in you, you are essentially poisoning yourself. Every time you have a negative emotion, you dispense small doses of poisonous chemicals within your body, and over time, this builds up in your physical body and creates disease. On the other hand, when you have positive, healthy and happy emotions, your body produces more feel good chemicals that help us to remain vibrant and alive, and stave off disease.

Every time you regurgitate an experience from your past, you bring those same physical sensations and negative emotions up in your body again, and again. Your body and your mind can't tell the difference between the thought of something, and the actual happening of something. So every time you replay the old memories of the past, you basically reinfect your body and mind with the poison of the experience. You do this over and over and over. Trust me, I have done this to myself many times in the past and I have found that it no longer serves me. Am I totally done with rehashing old memories and feeling bad about them? Heck no. This is a process. What I can tell you, is that with practice, it will become easier. You will need to use the experiences of your past as stepping stones instead of allowing them to be quicksand that sucks you into the depths of despair.

If old hurtful memories arise, try to think of something positive it pushed you towards. This can cement the idea in your subconscious mind that things are truly always working out for the best. When I was a teenager and my grandmother passed away, I was devastated that none of my local relatives were willing to take on the task of raising me. The only family willing to take me were some cousins that lived an hour and a half away. I was forced to move from the city I grew up in, away from everything I had ever known. Away from all my friends and all things familiar. Not only had I lost my grandmother, but as I saw it at the time, my entire existence.

Looking back on things now, I can see how I was guided to a much better place. Even though it didn't work out living with my relatives and I did end up in foster care, I look back on all those hardships with immense gratitude. I have allowed these experiences and numerous others to shape and mold me into a strong, powerful, loving, compassionate human being. Am I perfect, absolutely not! But you can be bitter, or you can be better. I certainly could have harbored resentment toward the people and circumstances that I experienced, but what I have found is that by letting go of all the past hurts and resentments, I have the capacity for Love and peace in my life. I wouldn't have it any other way.

I had heard for many years that in order to live your best life you had to be present, to live in the now. Be in this moment. I never really understood what they meant by that. After many years of searching, I now have a better understanding of what that means, and how to bring myself back when I find my mind has drifted away from my physical body. When your mind is not on the task at hand, it is away from you. Literally. It's like your mind goes on trips all day long. When you find yourself in a thought that has nothing to do with what you are currently in the middle of, your mind is on a mini vacation.

Learning to Love Yourself

It has left you. Your mind essentially abandons your body, and it is your job to retrieve it. Your mind can be on a vacation or it can be off to war. The breath is the most effective way to bring the mind back home.

Once you notice your mind is not on the task at hand, take a deep breath and recite a catchphrase or mantra of your choosing. One I really like a lot is from the book *The Big Leap* by Gay Hendricks: "I expand in abundance, success and love every day as I inspire those around me to do the same." As you can imagine, I say this a lot. Not as much as I did in the beginning, but my mind still has a tendency to forget where it lives, and I have to go out looking for it. Another reminder I have been telling myself is to "Enjoy this moment, because you can enjoy the other moments when you get there."

There is a whole Universe of available thoughts for your mind to think, and it wants to test out every scenario for itself. Have you ever created a story in your head, and thought, OH, my God, where did THAT come from??? I certainly have. I can start off with a small thought like, I have to return something at the store, and then my mind pulls in a thought of "Well what if they give you a hard time? Oh, well I will just tell them I will never shop there again if they don't take this back, and I will tell all my friends not to shop there and yadayadayada!!" This happens to me all the time, and I bet it happens to you too.

The best way to alleviate this is to develop your call to home. I remember when I was a kid and my Grammie wanted me to come home. She would go out on the back porch and call my name out into the neighborhood: "Jilllllll, Jilllllll, Jillll, it's time to come hooommmmeeee!" (Long before cell phones, LOL.) It's kind of like that. Your catch phrase or mantra will be a call to come home for your mind. Whenever you catch your ego going off on a joy ride, you will bring it back by reciting your favorite mantra. It will remind your conscious self it's time to come home.

Chapter 3

Ego

It is often suggested that in order to grow or succeed in life, one must give up the ego. It is my belief that we must not kill, do away with or destroy the ego, but one must cultivate the ego into a healthy rendition of one's unique identity. I actually do not believe it is possible to rid yourself of the ego. It would be like cutting off a limb. The purpose of the ego is to give us our individuality.

You see, the ego is the mechanism by which the Universe is able to expand. We are all part of the One, the whole Universe. The Universe is in us, and we are in the Universe. The ego allows the Universe the ability to expand in many directions, and for each soul to have the sense of differentiation, while still allowing it to be connected to Itself. Kind of like being on a life line back to home.

The biggest challenge with the ego as I see it, is that it has the capacity of free will. The propensity of the ego to want to be more important than the collective Whole is the real issue. When the ego is healthy, it will recognize the value and the good in the self. A person with a healthy ego is one who feels loving and kind and forgiving to oneself and others. Living with compassion and empathy. A healthy ego can see itself in the other person. A person whose ego is fragile and unhealthy will hold onto anger, reject others points of view and fail to thrive emotionally. Self-loathing is a sign of an ego in need of nurture and healing. The good news is that it is possible for the ego to heal.

If one has a healthy ego, one will make a mistake, recognize it as such, move on and learn from it. If you have a healthy ego, you will have compassion for yourself, just as you would with someone else. When a mistake is made, there is no self-loathing, no condemnation and no guilt. By the same token, one with a healthy ego will also be able to love and forgive others that have made mistakes and offer them compassion. No matter the perceived enormity of whatever action has been committed.

The ego does not want to allow us to let go of the thoughts that are upsetting to us, because it makes us feel as though we have lost our sense of identity. Where would the ego be without all the attachments? Where are we and who are we without the stories that we generated along the way? When we let go of all the fear, the anger, the frustrations and the memories, the ego feels threatened. Initially, when you try to let go of it all, you can be at peace for a few moments, but the ego floods it all back in so that your ego does not lose its sense of identity. I have come to realize though, that with consistent practice we can allow ourselves to let go of all the hurt, anger, fear, frustration and negative, unpleasant feelings, we can be at peace. It doesn't matter what happened to us in the past. If we can let go, we are at peace and that feels like success to me. The aim is to practice this consistently. The more often you attempt to bring yourself back from the past or future, the better you get at it. If you are not ruminating over the past and allowing the thoughts of past hurts and frustrations to settle in, you are free to enjoy the present moment. As I let go of the thoughts of the past, I am free to enjoy this sip of delicious coffee. I am free to enjoy seeing my cats interact and watch the birds enjoying the seed at the feeder. I am free to appreciate the comfortable seat I am sitting on. When we are free of the thoughts of the past and free of the mental projection of the future, we are free to enjoy whatever is going on right now. If we are working, we are more free to focus on the task at hand, and without past or future distractions, we are far more likely to do our best at what we are currently working on. If we are doing something for fun, we are more able to appreciate the fullness of the experience. Clinging to the past and trying to control the future with mental projection only serves to rob us of the experience that is happening RIGHT NOW!

When we are connected to our true nature, our inner being, we are able to hear the silence that surrounds the noise. It is possible to be in a room full of sounds and be able to connect to the silence that is present outside the noise.

To be connected to the Higher self, is to be totally present. When you are present, you can know there is no separation from anyone or anything. Everything emanates from the original source, our true essence, and our true essence is Love. The experience of creation was born of the desire of source energy to have physical experiences. When you feel the Source energy within you, you understand that it is formless and without physical senses. The desire of Source is to experience and create. Expansion of Source energy is why the physical realm exists.

With each birth, Source energy is able to have new and unique experiences. When the physical body expires, the energy that was emitted from Source energy returns to itself. Therefore, there is truly no separation and there is no death.

You are not what happened to you. Any negative or unpleasant events that have happened in the past are a part of the story that you are writing. The hero's journey. You have the ability to write an amazing outcome for yourself.

You are what you choose to be. You have a new choice each and every moment. You could be on a path of destruction and do terrible horrible things, and in an instant, you can choose a new path. You can realize when you've hurt someone, and choose to do better. You can make it your focus to help others. You can make it your focus to thrive and succeed and to be the best that you can possibly be. Every new moment is a new chance, every new moment holds the potential for greatness.

Chapter 4

Consciousness

The meaning of consciousness has always been somewhat of a vague concept to me. People would speak of Consciousness in a spiritual context and allude to the divine nature of Consciousness, but I didn't quite understand.

I knew that being conscious meant not sleeping and of being aware of your surroundings, but that is where it stalled for me.

I have since come to understand that thoughts are not actually generated in the brain. Thoughts are only processed by the brain. Therefore, thoughts are consciousness and Consciousness comes from somewhere outside the body and the brain.

Pure consciousness is above the level of the mind where you are able to observe everything around you without attaching meaning or thought to it. It is pure awareness. You are aware of everything, without giving anything a label or contemplating anything about it. No judgment. No thought. Just seeing things as they are. Nothing more. It's when we are in the now, the present moment, that we escape the matrix. No thoughts of past, no thoughts of future, but just being. Observing this moment, not judging the moment, but just experiencing it.

We all have moments of pure consciousness at times. We are just not aware that we are not having thoughts of anything. Have you ever had a moment when you were just staring out the window and not thinking of anything at all? These are the moments of pure consciousness. If you think back on those moments, I think you will recall how free, easy and blissful it felt.

There are levels of consciousness. One level is pure consciousness, then there is individual consciousness and collective consciousness:

Pure Consciousness: The deepest level, where there's a sense of simply *being* without any thoughts or boundaries. It's often described as a state of pure awareness or connection to the universe.

Individual Consciousness: About personal awareness, where we experience our own thoughts, emotions, and identity. It's the sense of "I" that we each feel, our unique perspective on the world.

Collective Consciousness: A shared level where individual minds connect with others. It includes shared beliefs, culture, and ideas that we all contribute to and are influenced by in return. This level affects how we interact with each other and shape society.

Each layer interacts with the world in different ways, from a universal awareness in pure consciousness to personal experiences in individual consciousness, all the way to societal influence in collective consciousness.

I am sure you have had the experience of having a thought or unfathomable story just randomly appear in your mind. Then you ask yourself, "Where the heck did THAT come from???" Well, the reason this happens is because our minds are connected to infinite consciousness. We have access to all the thoughts ever thought and ever to be thought. There are times when we are not in the moment, not paying attention and the thoughts just flood our minds playfully, randomly and sometimes overwhelmingly.

This realization solidified for me the belief that we are spiritual entities having a bodily experience. If the thoughts do not come from the mind, they must come from somewhere. It is from the Divine God soup so to speak that all these thoughts come from. From higher Consciousness. This human experience is limitless. Defined and limited only by the thoughts we think at each moment.

I had watched an interview on *Impact Theory*, a show hosted by Tom Bilyeu, with Deepak Chopra. He said something that profoundly impacted my thinking. He said he had at one point wanted to know what the source of knowing is. You see, you can find knowledge anywhere. You can get it from books, videos, YouTube, etc. But where does all the knowledge come from???

Consciousness

There are certain things we are born instinctively knowing, and how do we know them??? We know them, because we have always known them. We came into this world with all the knowledge that exists. It is merely hidden from our present level of human consciousness. We all possess within us all the knowledge that always has been and ever will be. It is often referred to as the Akashic records. If you just imagine you are looking for the solution to an issue that has come up in your life, you go into your mind and you sort and you sift through your mind until you find the answer. Where was that solution? It was in the records. Because whatever you are going through right now has already been gone through at some point in the history of the universe. It is our job in this present time, in this lifetime to seek out those answers and to put them into action. We are all just having a new experience every day and we depend on the past experiences of the universe to help us through what it is that we are experiencing now in this lifetime.

The greatest thing about all this is that we have the ability to think a different thought at any time!!! Every moment provides us the ability to think something other than what we had been previously thinking. If I was thinking "my life is so sad, I am depressed, I have nothing," I can say "wait a minute, is this really how I want to be thinking??? Is there something else I could be thinking instead???" I could think, "Things are hard at the moment, but I know with persistence and practice, my life can improve."

This takes work and practice, because our ego minds like to keep us stuck. The main purpose of the ego mind is to create a sense of individuality, so higher Consciousness can experience physical life from an infinite number of possibilities. The problem being is that somewhere along the way, the ego mind grew and developed a false sense of being of more importance than the collective consciousness.

The ego mind will generate negative thoughts to prevent you from connecting with higher consciousness. It will generate negative thoughts about yourself, about other people, about experiences. It will do whatever it takes to keep you from realizing your true higher nature.

For if you become aware of your true nature, your true connection with all that is, the ego feels threatened. The ego feels that you will no longer be special, unique, or different if you are just a part of some giant pot of soul soup.

But the true reality is that your unique life experiences lived through the ego are precisely what allows the universe to expand. Every moment of your life contributes to the Akashic records. The library of every thought, experience, emotion that has been or ever will be experienced. Your life, YOU, are unique, necessary, and in fact VITAL to the evolution of Higher Consciousness. GOD. You contribute to the growth and expansion of God. You are God and God is you.

Because of this, you have access to all the experiences and thoughts ever created. Our problem is we limit ourselves from accessing the knowledge available to us. We think that understanding, knowing and communicating with the higher realms is limited to a select few. The mediums, sages and seers. The truth is that we all have access to everything. In order to access this, we need to first come to the understanding that it is available to us, and then to practice letting it come in.

It sounds simple in theory. However, we have been conditioned by society and past experiences to deny and therefore block out the availability of this information. Like anything in life, it will take practice to hone these skills and to open up to the knowledge available to us.

If you have ever had a psychic reading that has really resonated with you, you understand that the information is accessible. The person providing the information has developed an open channel to the library. Some mediums are more connected than others. We all have this ability, though.

Your ego is valuable, it is necessary, it is just not more important than the true Essence that all the information arises from, and that is what it fears. The ego mind is a tool utilized by the Universe to help shape our experiences. The problem is, though, that we over use the ego mind. We allow it to run rampant. We let it constantly focus on experiences of the past or reach forward to thinking about how the future will play out. We can, with practice, notice when we are recalling the past or projecting the future. When you notice this, bring your focus back to the present moment. When you are in the present moment, you are observing what is happening right now. Right now is truly the only time that exists. It is essential for mental peace and clarity to focus in this moment. The more often you do this, the better you will get at it, and you will feel free and light.

Another concept of consciousness that occurred to me is that we are all experiencing our own individual realities. Like strands on a head of hair. We are all connected at the root, but we are all experiencing life from our own unique perspective and point of view. And when I say point of view, I mean that literally. Each of us from where we stand, experience reality. No two people can occupy the same space, therefore, we cannot see exactly what another person sees.

We can see things from a similar vantage point and have agreement on some aspects, but I do not, cannot and will never see things from your personal perspective.

I also cannot think your thoughts. Your thoughts create your reality and your view of the world, therefore, whatever you think is correct for you. You always have the ability to change your thoughts and point of view. You can change your beliefs, but I can never do that for you. I may have influence by providing you with my perspective, but it is up to you whether or not you accept or reject it.

The secret to the Universe is belief. We all live in the world according to our beliefs. Whatever I believe is true for me, and whatever you believe is true for you. If I believe I have a soul tribe, or that

I am able to connect with my loved ones across the veil, then it is so, and my experience will demonstrate that. If you believe there is no higher power, then for you that will also be true. You are creating your experience by the things that you believe and think. The most amazing thing is, we can always change what we think and believe. A belief is just a thought that you think over and over. This is why repetition of affirmations is so effective. If you say it over and over, believe it and feel it, it will be true for you. Think about the fact that a habitual liar eventually ends up believing their own lies. Their lies end up being their truth, and there is no convincing them otherwise. You have the power and ability to use repetition of positive statements and mantras for the benefit of your own life.

There can be, and are, groups of people who think common thoughts and they tend to band together and create a collective worldly consciousness. They repeat their ideas, dogma and beliefs, emphatically and religiously until they are drilled into people's conscious experience. Since this is the case, wouldn't it make sense to input ideas that are healthy, loving and serving humanity? Why would anyone want to dwell upon or absorb ideas that are harmful, hurtful, or mean? If you truly want peace in your life, you need to choose the ideas and concepts that promote peace, love and kindness. If you are going to choose your experience, why not make it a good one?

We have different political factions, religious sects, and other cultural groups. We have so many cultural divides. There are racial divides, religious divides, political divides, gender divides, economic divides, and so many others.

These groups of people collectively agree upon how life is and how it should be, and for them, it is so. The big trouble with many of these factions is that they erroneously believe that their way is the only way. Sometimes these people take great actions to try to influence how you believe. They try to force their ideas and beliefs on others with great pressure. If we could all open our minds to accept that what is true for yourself and your collective, is not how it is for everyone, we would not have the need for wars, protests and violence. We are all here to experience life differently, and endeavoring to force your ideas and beliefs on another only creates discord.

Now, I am not suggesting that if you have an idea or opinion on something you don't share it with others. That is exactly what I am doing with this book. I am merely suggesting that you are not tied to the need for the other person or group of people accepting the belief that you share. I would love for this book to be a catalyst for change in the lives of those who read it, but if no one likes it, or thinks my ideas are not for them or worthwhile, I am not upset by that. This is my worldview, I am living my world, my experience, and if by sharing it, you benefit, I am happy for that, but if you discard it, I am still happy either way.

Consciousness

The need to control others is an ego construct. I have found in my life that the more I let go of the outcome of a situation, the more at peace I am. I have had to practice diligently on this, as it is human/ego nature to be driven to control the outcome of all situations.

Chapter 5

Feelings

All feelings come from within. Whether it is happiness, anger, sadness, boredom, intrigue, fear, or any other feeling you may have. Your thoughts generate the feelings in your body. Outside influences can play a role in your feelings in that when an experience occurs, you have a thought about it, and then a feeling arises in you about the thought you had of that experience. But ultimately, the feeling is created in your body by the thought that arises. Outward expressions of feelings also have inner feedback. When you are angry and yell out at someone, inside your body the chemical adrenaline is released. This is the "fight or flight chemical". When people are angry and yelling all the time and constantly stressed, it can lead to a range of negative effects on the body, including increased blood pressure, heart strain, anxiety, difficulty sleeping, muscle tension, and potentially increased risk of heart disease or stroke. Truly, your anger is killing you. The same is true for positive feelings. When you are feeling good, your body primarily releases chemicals like dopamine, serotonin, and endorphins which are often referred to as "feel-good" hormones; dopamine is associated with pleasure and reward, serotonin contributes to overall well-being, and endorphins act as natural pain relievers and can produce feelings of euphoria. So your peace and well-being contribute to wellness within the body.

You have the ability to create any feeling you would like to have by creating a thought about it in your mind. With this knowledge, you would think that more people would just choose to be happy and think happy thoughts all the time. The challenge with this is that the subconscious mind is the primary driver of most of our thoughts. We have many thousands of thoughts on any given day, and a majority of those thoughts are the same thoughts we've had the day before. With this in mind, you can imagine how challenging it can be to intentionally choose a positive thought. But this is exactly what we must do to make improvements in our feelings, moods and experiences.

In order to make changes in your life, you have to stop living your life on autopilot, you need to set your intentions. If you are looking to feel happy, you can create that feeling intentionally. I have found that if I sit still with my eyes closed and take a few deep breaths to calm myself, I can then look around within myself. I look for happiness as if I were looking for a pair of shoes or some lost item. You can do this with whatever emotion you wish to experience. You can do it with positive emotions and their opposites.

So with my eyes closed, I can think of the word happiness. Then I say to myself, "where is happiness inside myself?" Then I "look" and then the feeling grows within me. I say "Ah, there it is!" You will be able to experience this with very little effort at all. It just takes concentrated thought. Or, you can ask yourself the question "What does happiness feel like?" Close your eyes and allow yourself to feel it. It will come. I promise you. If you are intentional about it, give it a sincere effort and have an open mind, the feeling WILL arise.

This will help you feel the concept of happiness being within you. It is part of your very nature. The things outside you can bring happiness. But this type of happiness is transitory. When someone does something nice for you, or you buy something nice that you have been wanting, sure, you will feel happy for a time. But, that feeling will fade all too quickly. When you develop the practice of feeling the happiness inside you, you can call on it whenever you need. This is not to say you will remember to do this all the time, but as with anything worthwhile, you will need to do it over and over and over.

Just think of a pro athlete. They practice their craft constantly. When they take time off, and come back, it takes them a while of practice again to get back to their peak performance. The same is true for you and me, and for anyone who aims to have pro-

Feelings

ficiency at anything at all in life. I don't care if it is sports, arts & crafts, singing, standing on your head, or whatever. You need to practice it. The same goes for happiness, forgiveness, love, honesty, compassion, you need to focus on these things daily, or you lose the vibrancy of the emotion. It still runs in the background, but the capacity to express these things becomes less intense.

You must also realize that wherever you go, there you are. What do I mean by this? You need to resolve the inner struggles you carry within yourself or not matter where you go you are going to encounter the same issues over and over again in your life. You will recreate the same issues with different people and surroundings until you learn that the issues lie within you and in your own mind.

If you are in an abusive relationship, whether it be physical or emotional, you must understand that something within you deep down must feel as though you are unworthy of love, or that you are innately flawed or bad and deserve to be treated poorly.

We are conditioned as children, and the lessons we learn from birth through age six are deeply ingrained in our subconscious mind. This is your programming. If you were repeatedly told as a child that you are bad, or annoying, or not good enough in any way, you will internalize those falsehoods as truth. You will take these false impressions with you into your relationships. Also, if you grow up in a household that was tumultuous, uncaring or otherwise unstable, it is most common for children to feel somehow they are to blame for the chaos or discord. Of course this is not the case, but the child's mind does not have the capability to understand this.

Once you realize you are in an unhealthy relationship, you will need to first separate yourself from the abuse, but then, you will need to work on the part of you that has been deceived. You must learn your true perfect nature and learn to love yourself. You are a whole, perfect being of love and light.

When you find yourself in a situation with another person who is demonstrating negative energy toward you or just in general, it will be helpful to remember that you can at any point make a conscious choice to remain calm. The words another person says can only hurt you if you take offense. If you remain calm, you win. As my good friend Lilly Wang once told me, "The strongest energy in the room wins!"

I am not saying this is easy. I am saying that with practice, it will be possible to disregard a negative onslaught from an energy source that is unconscious and out of control. People are negative and hurt others out of pure ignorance and lack of self-control. No matter where you are, the strongest energy in the room wins. If you join the other person in their negative energy space, you both lose. You have the ability, with practice, to generate a more powerful energy field and thus neutralize a negative situation.

If you feel you are not capable at the moment, you may find it more beneficial to remove yourself from the situation until you have more practice and

Feelings

energy to rise to the challenge. But, know that you are capable, and have compassion for yourself even if you aren't able to do it in the current moment. With practice, you will get better at it.

One concept that I had a hard time wrapping my mind around is being OK with not being OK. We all have times in our lives when things are not going well, could be going totally bonkers, or is downright totally shitty. We feel upset and try as hard as we can to fight the feelings we are experiencing, when in reality, the best thing we could do to heal is to allow ourselves to feel the uncomfortable feelings until they subside. I know for myself, when I am feeling sad, anxious or upset, I feel it in my gut and in the middle of my chest. This would be why I have suffered with stomach issues for many years. When I accept what is going on, and allow myself to experience the hurt without judging myself, the pain subsides much quicker than if I fight it. Be like water and flow with the experience.

Everything is as it should be. I tell myself, "I am grateful for all that I am, for all that I have, for all that I do, and for the love and peace that dwells within me." This reminder for me is very beneficial in bringing myself back to a place where I can feel OK with whatever I may be experiencing.

As true as all this is, there are sometimes in our lives when we need a little help through the times when we are not OK, and we need to honor this. Recognize that it is not a sign of weakness to ask for or seek help. Whether it is help from a friend or a qualified professional, looking for guidance is one of the wisest and strongest things a person can do. The ego lies to us and tells us we are weak if we seek help from an outside source. When I am having a time where I feel like outside influences are clouding my judgment and I am ruminating on issues occurring in my life, I will reach out to my therapist and schedule a tune-up session. I value the outside perspective of the challenges I am having. She always gives me great insights and an open space to express all my frustrations and work on them in a healthy manner.

Some people view being vulnerable as a weakness. From my perspective, being vulnerable and honest with people is actually a great strength. It is the people who hide their feelings and emotions behind a tough facade that end up miserable and dysfunctional.

People who don't allow themselves to feel their emotions, just keep stuffing them down inside until they eventually can't stuff it anymore and explode. Crying is NOT a sign of weakness, it is the body's natural pressure release valve. I believe that if more people would allow the tears instead of suppressing them, there would be so much less anxiety plaguing society.

When we are stuck in a pattern of despair or unease, we can get locked into our limited way of looking at the world. An outside guide can offer different perspectives that can totally shift the way you experience life.

Feelings

When my daughter passed, I was of course devastated. I spent many months feeling numb and unmotivated. She passed in August of 2021, and by December, I knew I needed to seek professional support. The universe guided me to an amazing therapist Sarah Dionne who compassionately helped me work through grief, self-doubt, and fear. With her expert guidance I was able to accept the reality of a different relationship with my daughter and to treat myself with compassion. As with any tragedy in life, I will forever be different and coming to terms with that has made it much easier to navigate.

CHAPTER 6

Fuel for the Body and Soul

Learning is a gift. Everything you learn has the potential to evolve into something magnificent, and the best part of learning is being able to share what you have learned with others. Whether that is in teaching it to others, or by producing a product that benefits others, sharing your knowledge is not only essential, it is one of the most rewarding aspects of life. It is by sharing what you know and what you have learned with others that we become immortal. Our legacy lives on in the lives of those we touch.

Everything in life is meant to be experienced. This is why we are here, so consciousness can experience and create.

The food we eat is meant to be experienced. It is meant to be tasted, savored and appreciated. When you take a bite of an apple, notice the texture, the juiciness, the flavor. Experience the chewing and the swallowing. Experience the act of eating the apple. When you have a hot meal, smell the aroma of the food. With each bite, see how many flavors you can detect in the food you are eating. Do you notice the garlic or the pepper? How about the saltiness? Is it too much, just right? What about the dessert? Is it sweet? Creamy? Cake? The more you experience your food, the more satisfied you will be and in turn the less desire you will have to overeat.

One thing to also note, is that when eating, digestion begins in the mouth. As we start to chew our food, the body releases enzymes in the mouth, and signals enzymes in the gut to process the types of foods we are eating. If you rush through eating your food and don't fully chew it, the body may not release enough of the enzymes necessary to adequately process your food for proper nutritional uptake. In other words, your body will not absorb the nutrients optimally if you don't break it down enough.

This is why I believe drinking shakes consistently instead of properly consuming a nutritious meal can interfere with nutrient absorption. Sure, if you need to occasionally when you are on the go and when you are in a hurry, have a shake, but I believe there is no substitute for a balanced meal.

We need to be good stewards of the bodies we have been entrusted to care for. We always have the choice of the types of foods we eat or avoid, the types of activities we engage in. We also have the choice to not to engage at all. It is up to you to make the right choice for your body. The body is our home, don't you want to take care of the place you live?

The body is made up of a community of cells that we have an obligation to care for and nurture. Much like a president has the obligation to do all that it can to care for and provide for the citizens, we must treat our bodies as well as we can. If we eat good food, exercise, meditate and do what we can to promote wellbeing, our bodies will respond in kind. If we treat the body poorly, it will respond by breaking down and you will feel unwell, and miserable. We have been provided with wonderful resources to nourish our bodies, but in the fast paced life we are living, it has become far too convenient to ingest processed foods that lack the nutrition our bodies crave and deserve. Something the Indian mystic Sadhguru said that really resonated with me is that if we eat food that is dead, it does not provide us with nutrition. Things like fried foods and processed foods. Eating live plants provides us with life-giving energy. Vegetables and fruits should make up the largest portion of our nutrition. When you eat a food that is fried, processed or packaged, it has essentially been stripped of all of the nutrition. As I see it, we really need to reconsider what goes into our mouths. Much of the food supplies have been tainted with chemicals, dyes, and genetically altered material that have no business in the human body.

Chapter 7

Masks

The true self is cloaked by the mask of the physical body. If the mask falls away, our spiritual connected nature is revealed. The body is an illusion. Manifested from universal energy, concentrate into physical form, to rise up to be able to have experiences.

Every morning, we get up to begin a new day, and we put on the mask we will show the world. Some people put on very heavy masks that hide who they truly are, and some people put on a lighter mask that is closer to what lies beneath.

No matter who you are, if you get dressed in the morning, you are wearing a mask. Even the monks who adorn simple robes are donning a mask. What we really need to do as humans is to recognize the mask and honor the true self and nature beneath that mask.

I am nothing and everything at the same time. From the space of my pure essence, I am nothing, and I expand out from that center into everything. You do the same, and my pure essence intertwines with your pure essence and the pure essence of all beings is connected. This is Universe. This is Oneness. If I am emitting energy, and you are sitting next to me emitting energy, those energies don't bounce off each other, they mix together like a recipe. We are co-creating. This is the God Soup. The Oneness. There is no separation. We are all One entity composed of an infinite number of cells. Just like the human body is composed of trillions of cells, we can consider our individual life experience as a Universal cell. We are all part of the Whole.

Our beliefs are just another layer of our masks. The things we believe shape our experiences and determine the paths we take in life. It is my firm belief that there are no bad decisions in life. There are only decisions, and the outcome of those decisions determine where it is that we go next.

If we make a decision and we don't like the outcome, we can make a new decision. Ultimately the winding path of decisions we make, shapes our experience. We always have the choice to make a new decision or to change a belief. The simple act of deciding to take a different route to work in the morning can have a profound impact on the trajectory of your life going forward. Say you take a different street because the traffic will be better that way and you find out later you avoided a terrible accident, or say you take that route and you get into a terrible accident. Either way your life has taken a new direction. Say you did have the accident, what happens from there is all up to you. How you process the information from that experience will give you immeasurable options to consider. Which hospital will you go to, which doctor will you use, will you be an advocate for your health care or will you rely on the information you are exposed to? Every moment of every day is a blip in a long series of decisions. From the time you wake up, to the food you put in your mouth, to the words you choose to speak or not speak. Every moment can be a turning point in your life.

If you want to live your best life, it is important to connect with your true nature. Rely on Divine guidance. You may not always understand or appreciate where you are guided, but if you have faith that Divine wisdom is guiding you, you can be free to let go of the fear that drives us to anxiety and destructive thoughts. Take time to meditate, ask your higher guidance for direction and have faith that things always work out, even if it is not how we envisioned.

SCUBA—Self Contained Unique Body Apparatus

You've probably heard of scuba diving, but did you know that SCUBA stands for *Self-Contained Underwater Breathing Apparatus*? Now, think of your physical body as your own SCUBA gear—your *Self-Contained Unique Body Apparatus*—designed for exploring the earthly plane. Just as a diver relies on their equipment to explore the ocean, you rely on your body to navigate the world. A diver would never enter the water without filling their tank with air. Similarly, you should "fill your tank" each day with meditation, healthy nutrition, and exercise, preparing yourself for the day's journey just as a scuba diver prepares for an underwater adventure.

And just what is the purpose of all of this? Each life has its own unique experiences, and they are infinitely varied. Some are horrible and tragic, some are boring and uneventful, and some are exciting, abundant and pleasant. There are no limits and no end to the types of experiences that have been had, or that can ever be had.

As pure consciousness, a life experience is created and then lived out by the energy body experiencing the trajectory set into motion. We are given the ego to provide us with a sense of distinction, and we are given a set of circumstances to navigate. It is our job, goal, purpose to see what it is we can do with the life situations set before us. There will be varying degrees of life and living along the way.

I believe the end goal is to lead us back to source energy. I believe it is our life's purpose to experience all that we can and do it to the best of our ability, so that we can bring our experiences back with us. Each time we enter into a life, we have new and different experiences that enhance and expand higher Consciousness.

Masks

I also feel that as each experience comes back with us, every life we have ever lived, lives on in infinity. Each time we have an earthly experience, we connect with the conscious energy surrounding us at that moment of time and point of space, and it is forever entangled and remembered as we return to source energy. I believe this is why when we die, we are reconnected with our loved ones. And not just the loved ones of your current experience, but the energy of all the loved ones of all the experiences you have ever had. Which is to say, the whole of creation. The infinite universe.

Chapter 8

Spiritual Awakening

I had heard people speak of having a spiritual awakening. From the sounds of it, it was something that I aspired to experience in my life, however, I could not grasp the true idea of it, or how it could be manifest in my experience.

I believed it was possible though, and believing is the impetus driving you in the direction of spiritual growth and ultimately your awakening. It starts with belief and faith, and it can be revealed to you at literally any moment. There is a difference between believing in something and having an experience of something.

It was just over a year since my daughter Jenna's passing on that I came to experience this more enlightened state.

I am sure my entire life had been building to that moment. From birth and all the experiences in between. Each moment, good and seemingly otherwise, had been the building blocks for the moment I became truly aware of my connection to Higher Consciousness. It happened to occur however, just after a particularly miserable bout with Covid-19.

It had been a progressive sickness. Starting one evening just prior to bed with some unusual body aches. I tried to recall something I may have done to be experiencing the aches, but nothing came to mind. I just figured it would subside by the morning. Well, just a couple of hours later, I woke up with the feeling I might be sick. And indeed, I was, and violently. The illness progressed from there, and over the course of ten days I had a new symptom develop almost daily. When one symptom would subside, I got a new one. It felt miserable.

I was an emotional wreck, I cried a lot and had a big giant pity party. I felt so miserable and alone. I lived by myself with my three cats. No one to take care of me, no one to talk to. It was at this low point that the last nine years since my divorce all came rushing back at me. All the desperation and sadness, all the regret. Wishing things had turned out differently. It was a surreal experience.

About a week after having Covid, though, I had the most wonderful experience of my life. I had a spiritual awakening.

I had been in a particularly deep meditation when the realization of my oneness with Higher Consciousness became more than a belief. It became a deep knowing. I experienced a sense of connection that I had never known in my life before. At this point, I saw that even though I was physically by myself during Covid, I was NEVER alone. I have never been alone my whole life. I have always been connected to my Higher Consciousness. I was just unaware. For me, my spiritual awakening was simply becoming aware of my origin, of my true nature, of my inability to be separate. We are all connected at the deepest spiritual level. Each person has their own energy they are working with in this experience. Some have happy lighter energy and some have deep, heavy and unpleasant energy. But beyond all that, we are still connected. We are all light energy beings emanating from the same source. You are me and I am you. When I look at you, I am source energy looking out at myself from another vantage point. It is like looking in a mirror. Light is the highest form of perception. When we look at another and see their light, we are experiencing the true oneness.

I see now that we are here to experience life from an infinite number of perspectives. When one dies, they are not lost or gone. They have re-integrated with Higher Consciousness. Bringing along with them all the collective experience of that lifetime. Adding to the library of knowledge of all life experiences. The Akashic records. It is from this library that the myriad of seemingly random thoughts originates.

If you consider the number of thoughts that enter our minds each waking moment. You will have to ask yourself, *Where do all these thoughts come from?* They are not generated in the brain. They come from somewhere outside the brain. I am sure you have

Spiritual Awakening

experienced thoughts that you wondered where they came from. If there were no Akashic library there would be no way for people to have the multitude of infinite thoughts available to them. We are here to continually add to the library of the collective conscious experience. So you see, the library is not a physical place full of physical books. It is an infinite database of every thought that has ever been and every thought that will ever become. Higher consciousness is the Akashic records.

Chapter 9

Enlightenment

Enlightenment is a seemingly elusive state that all who venture on the spiritual journey strive for attainment, but no one can really articulate what Enlightenment truly is. From my understanding, it is indescribable. However, the best explanation I have come across thus far comes from the Vietnamese monk Thich Nhat Hanh. He says, "Enlightenment is when a wave realizes that it is the ocean." This description really resonates with my understanding; however, I would take it a little further. I would say that Enlightenment is when a wave realizes that it is the ocean and can recall that realization each time it crests. You see we are experiencing life on a human level, and we all typically interact with numerous people and circumstances throughout our everyday experiences. The challenge is, that not everyone we interact with in our daily lives are in line with our ideas, beliefs, wants and needs. Some

Enlightenment

experiences can be unpleasant and challenging, while others can be enriching and nurturing. These experiences can cause even enlightened beings to forget their true nature. From what I gather, in those I see as Enlightened beings is the understanding of your true nature and being able to maintain that understanding and sense of peace no matter who you are interacting with or what the circumstances are. I have not yet mastered this ability; however, I will continue to work toward that experience.

Chapter 10

Love

God is Love, Love is God, and Love is evolution. It is common in many religions for people to envision God as a man sitting on a throne with a long white robe, a beard and a golden staff or something along those lines. The concept I would like to introduce to you is that God is Love. More specifically, the energy of Love. Everything in the Universe is made up of energy and God is the original Source of that energy and that energy is Love. You can prove this to yourself by exploring the different energies of feelings within your own physical being. Any feeling you wish to conjure can be done so by the power of your thought. If you ask yourself what happiness feels like, close your eyes and focus on that, you can generate happiness in your body. You can ask yourself what jealousy feels like, close your eyes and focus, and I guarantee your energy will shift to a feeling that is uncomfortable and undesir-

Love

able. The feeling of Love is the ultimate high vibration. You won't find a feeling within you that feels better than that. Love is the underlying energy source of all that is. It is through Love that we evolve.

If you look hard enough you can find love in everything. The chair you are sitting in. Someone loved enough to create it. That person thought of the love of comfort and style and how the chair would function in your space. Your refrigerator is love. Someone loved food enough to want to preserve it and went to work to develop a way to store food for longer periods of time. The heating system in your home was created out of love. The carpet on your floor, the lotion you put on your hands, streetlights, stores, flowers, pets, and anything at all you can think of. Every invention, idea, and physical manifestation was born out of love. Love is at the core of everything. I ask you to challenge yourself to look around your space and choose any item and consider how it can be traced back to love. Even things that appear to be unpleasant, hurtful, or evil, in some way can be traced back to love. This is not to minimize the deep pain and suffering people endure, nor to suggest that the harm caused is ever justified. Instead, it asks us to consider the origins of even the darkest actions. Many acts of cruelty stem from fear, which is often the absence of love, or from a distorted form of love—love of power, love of control, or love of self above others. By tracing back to the root, we often find unmet needs for love, compassion, or understanding. While this awareness does not erase the harm, it opens a pathway to healing by seeking to understand and reclaim love in its purest form. This is not about excusing or condoning, but rather about transforming—transforming our own hearts in the face of hurt and offering the chance for love to guide us toward forgiveness, empathy, and growth.

Chapter 11

Physical Reality

Everything in this physical world emanates from one universal energy source. Some call it God, some call it ether, some call it spirit. No matter what you call it or what spiritual beliefs you have, it all comes down to energy. This energy moves forth and concentrates in varying degrees in various places to form our physical reality.

When two or more energies are combined, a new energy density is formed. Water is made of atoms arranged in a certain pattern. When water is combined with dirt it forms a new energy density. We call it mud. If mud is Combined with the energy of heat and air, it will form clay. Then the clay can be used to form a building. So it is with all other forms of energy combinations. When male and female reproductive energy combines, it forms a new energy density called an ovum. The ovum then combines with the energy density fed to it by the mother and it transforms into a baby. From birth until death, our energy form is constantly changing, in size, shape and composition. We transform from infancy to toddler, from toddler to child, from child to adolescent, from adolescent to young adult, from middle-age adult to senior citizen. From a senior citizen to a transcendent being. In death, our physical bodies continue to change. It decomposes from the physical life form it was and transforms into other varying degrees of energy. For instance, the gasses that are emitted from a decaying body are another form of energy. If left to mother nature and the earth, the body would become life energy for other forms of life, such as maggots and other bugs.

Energy can never die. It can only be transformed. This is why it is my firm belief that when the soul leaves the physical body it reintegrated with source energy. Coming home to share all the experiences of a lifetime. To contribute to the ever evolving/growing Akashic records.

Energy can be concentrated or dense, or energy can be light, airy and free. There can also be many levels in between. The energy of an immovable object is very concentrated or dense and is very slow moving. This is why the object appears solid. Lighter forms of energy are fast moving and more pliable. Animated energy is things that are alive and have motion. Like trees, plants, bugs, animals and humans. However, all energy is the same even though it moves at different speeds. Therefore everything and everybody is

Physical Reality

ultimately one giant pool of energy in-separable and united.

The way we manage the energy in our lives is extremely important. It is very important to organize the energy in our physical space as well as the energy in our spiritual and emotional environment.

When you have large amounts of clutter surrounding you, you may feel overwhelmed. This is because there is an energy density where it should be free flowing and light. If you put the clutter in a container, say a drawer or closet, the space will feel lighter and free. It is no longer affecting your physical space. If you see something on the floor that does not belong there, take a quick moment to pick it up and put it where it belongs. If it belongs to someone else, put it somewhere for them to take care of when they have a chance. It is so much easier to take care of something in the moment than to let it sit and fester. All of these little things create a healthy environment not only for living, but also for the emotions. It may seem silly, but simply making your bed in the morning has an impact on your day. Making your bed signifies you are complete with the sleep cycle, and allows you to enter the sleep cycle at the end of the day in a more organized fashion. Closing the door on the cabinets and closing drawers when you are done, keeps the energy of the contents from spilling into your living space. Closing the lid on the toilet before flushing keeps the bathroom environment more healthy and clear of the energy of waste. Things don't have to be perfect, but the more organized and clean our environment is, the more energy we have to concentrate on things that really matter.

We can also apply this concept to human energy. It can be overwhelming in large amounts. Have you ever been to a party and just felt overwhelmed and not really know why? This is because of the large amounts of energy co-mingling in a confined space. Not that the energy is necessarily bad, it can just be a lot and can feel overwhelming. This is especially true for empaths who tend to physically feel all the energy that surrounds them.

Personally, if I have to attend a large event, I prepare myself by accepting my limits and honoring my feelings. I am usually one of the first to arrive. This gives me time to adjust to the increasing volume of energies entering the space. I am happy to engage with as many people as I feel comfortable with and stay as long as I feel light, but if the energy builds too intensely, I will find a quieter space to release a little or politely make my exit. I am usually very clear upfront that I may leave a little early, that way people don't feel slighted when I excuse myself.

It's all about honoring yourself and knowing your limits. When we push too far beyond our set point, we can become irritable and create unease within the body. By allowing this to happen, we also open ourselves up to creating tension with those around us. We may not even be aware we are doing it.

We all have the ability to generate positive or negative build-up of energies within our bodies.

Physical Reality

Each individual uses their energy in their own unique fashion. This is why some people can utilize certain energy techniques better than others.

We all have within us a never-ending supply of energy. The amazing thing is we get to choose what type of energy it is that we are utilizing. When we focus on positive thoughts, we generate positive energy, and when we focus on negative thoughts, we generate negative energy within us. The choice is yours.

We all experience the energy of emotions, it is imperative that we stop and assess how we want to work with these energies. All of the energy of emotions is beneficial if we use it constructively. If we are feeling an uncomfortable emotion about something it is a signal from our higher self that something needs adjusting. Whether it is something within ourselves or something externally, it is important to utilize the uncomfortable energy for a peaceful resolution. Open your heart and feel the emotion and ask yourself if this is something coming from the ego self or an indication that there is an action you need to take to rectify an external influence.

If it is coming from within, it is beneficial to allow and accept the emotion, feel it for as long as you need to, and at some point, make a conscious decision to release it. If it is truly coming from an external injustice or circumstance, it is important for you to peacefully find the resources and avenues to take action to rectify the situation if possible. Sometimes we also need to accept the situation for what it is and allow it to play out without any interference from us. As hard as this may be sometimes, the sooner we let things go and accept them as they are, the sooner we can stop lamenting, plotting and judging over things. This wastes so much energy. It is exhausting. Once we allow ourselves to let go, we can use our energy for the things in life that are within our circle of influence.

We come into this life from the original Source energy, and as the journey begins, we are essentially leaving home. As we are born, we grow and travel further and further from our Source energy. We have many experiences along the way that cause us to forget where we came from. We forget the power that is within us. We have a lifeline to source energy and it is the feelings of Love within us. But the further away you go from the lifeline, the harder it is to see where you came from. However, as the circle of life goes, we come back around. We begin to see glimpses of where we came from and start to remember our true nature. I believe this is why people start to look for spirituality in midlife. As we age, and get closer and closer to the shoreline, the infinite source that we came from becomes significantly more prominent in our field of vision.

Chapter 12

Programming

Most, if not all, of our life circumstances and situations have a significant relationship to our subconscious programming. The way we were programmed as children has a direct effect on the way we live our lives, the choices we make and the people we attract into our lives.

Our subconscious mind is widely thought to be programmed from birth to age seven. I would suggest it begins prior to our physical entrance into this world. I believe that the way a mother experiences her reality while a baby is in utero has a direct effect on the programming of the child. The child can sense the feelings of the mother, and this has an impact on the life and personality of the child.

Our base programs are ingrained in us by age seven, but we are constantly being programmed. By everyone and everything that surrounds us. Television, movies, news, social media, our peers.

Heck, they even tell you they are programming you. If you look at a television guide it will tell you what program is on. You get to choose the programs you watch. You get to choose the social media you invest your time in. You get to choose the books you read, the friends you associate with and the people you allow to remain in your life. You ultimately, in fact, do create your own reality.

If you want a better life, you need to choose better programming, and you must do this consistently. Quite some time ago, I decided to give up mainstream television. I no longer watch prime time television.

A few years back, I got sucked into a show called *This Is Us*. It was a captivating drama of a family whose father had died when the kids were just teens. It detailed the lives they lived prior to his death, and flashed back and forth to various time periods in the lives of these people from past, present and future. It was very well written and always had a storyline that sucked you right in. It was, as they say, binge worthy. But what I realized from watching this show is that their drama was stressing me out. You see, your brain does not know the difference between fact & fiction. It only knows what you input into it. Garbage in garbage out as they say. I would notice after a particularly thrilling episode, I would ruminate over it for days. Trying to figure out how the characters were going to deal with the scenario, how would I deal with it if it were me, and worried about how they

Programming

would make it through this particular thing. It was affecting my emotional well-being.

With so many programs available on oodles of various media channels, it is no wonder that the dominant plague of society today is stress. You almost can't go anywhere these days without being bombarded with programming. From hundreds of news outlets, social media channels, email blasts, tabloids, streaming services, and God knows what else. We are unconsciously and consistently giving up our emotional freedom.

The best way to get some relief from this constant bombardment of negativity and drama is to make a conscious choice of what we read, watch and expose ourselves to. For me personally, I canceled my cable television service, found a streaming service called Gaia that focuses on health, spirituality and metaphysics, and found some teachers that resonate with me on YouTube and subscribed to their channels. This way, I am choosing my programming. I get to decide the content that fills my thoughts. The better the input, the better the output.

If we are born into lives of fear, trauma and negativity, it would make sense that we would find it challenging to overcome what seems to be an ordinary way of life. If you grow up in a family where there is constant bickering, arguing and yelling, it would feel somewhat normal to witness this on a daily basis. However, our true nature, the one that knows true love and higher consciousness, is well aware this is not how things are intended to be. We understand on a deeper level that something is not right, but we are torn between the comfort of the familiar and the fear of the unknown.

It takes great courage to break out of this type of mold. But I assure you that when you finally do, you will wonder why it took so long.

It is very important to consciously and continuously be generating positive energy in your life. Even though we have an infinite supply of energy, our bodies can only hold so much at one time. Kind of like a rechargeable battery. At the beginning of the day, we are renewed and energized, but we use the energy throughout the day and are depleted by the end of the day. We can take breaks throughout the day and recharge, but the full recharge is our nightly sleep cycle. This is why sleep is so important. It is our daily renewal.

I have multiple energy practices I employ in my morning routine. I find that these practices set my day off in the right direction.

I begin the day with stretching my body. I find this gets all my muscles and joints fluid again after a long night of sleep. The fluids in the body become viscous as we sleep, and we need movement to get things flowing. From there I have my prayers and gratitude practice, my affirmations and meditation, and I have a practice that involves the moving of chi in the body (the circulating life force of the body).

While these practices do take a bit of time each morning, I find that they give me a sense of balance and control over my life that make it worth the effort.

Programming

I had considered at one point if I were spending too much time in the morning on my energy practices, however, when I considered the positive energy production, it made sense to me. The energy that flows into your home comes from a powerplant that is constantly producing energy, if the flow of that energy is disrupted, there is no more electricity. If we cease to create positive energy within ourselves consistently, it can be very easy to slip into old negative patterns and be depleted. The better we get at creating our energy consciously, the more beautiful and abundant lives we create.

CHAPTER 13

Words

The words we speak produce the reality we experience. As a magician speaks the word *Abracadabra*—"As I speak, so it is!"—you must also speak your reality into form. Make it a practice to shift your language to incorporate positivity and expressions of the life you want. If you continuously lament the circumstances of your life, you will continue to experience those same circumstances over and over again. If you can shift your language to an idea of positive transition, you can improve your situation dramatically.

Consider that every time you complain, you are reinforcing the energy of things to complain about. If you complain about your job, your family, your friends, or anything else in your life, you will remain stuck in situations that are uncomfortable or unpleasant.

Words

If you have a situation in your life that is less than ideal, try to be aware of how you explain it or interpret it to others. Instead of saying "my boss is a jerk," try something a little lighter like "I am working on navigating the energy my boss is emitting." This puts the power in your hands. Instead of saying "I am having a bad day," try saying, "I am having a moment that I am not enjoying," because really a whole day is rarely, if ever, entirely bad. There may be parts of a day that are awful, or that things don't go as expected, but there is something good in even the worst of days. Simply waking up and noticing you are breathing is a blessing. Even when life feels overwhelming and like the world is crashing down on you, if you make the effort to find something to be thankful for, it will give you the strength and courage to move forward, beyond whatever it is that feels hurtful at this moment.

It is your tenacity and grit in troubling times that fuel your propulsion to a better life situation.

Make it a practice to set your life's intentions. The vast majority of people float along through life allowing the outside circumstances dictate the course their ship is sailing. It never occurs to them to take control of the sail. If you take off from the shore without setting the sail, you can end up anywhere. It could be somewhere you enjoy, or perhaps not. Setting your intentions is like setting the sail of your ship. No longer being tossed about aimlessly. You will not escape the storms, because life is full of them, however, if you consistently adjust your sails toward a defined destination, you will eventually get there.

Your intentions can always change and you will have to readjust your course, but this is the magnificent part of the journey.

Say for some reason you lose your job or end a relationship. This can have a devastating impact on your life situation; however, you do not have to let the circumstance dominate your life. First, you must allow yourself to move through the feelings of the loss. Cry, yell, lament, meditate, or do whatever it takes to release the hurt. Anytime something beyond our control affects our life, we have lost a measure of security and stability. You must deal with the feeling of loss, because if you don't, it will sink into the body and create a concentration of unhealthy stagnant energy somewhere within. We all have these pockets of stuck stagnant energy in our physical bodies. It is from the practice of stuffing down hurt, anger and frustrations that we become ill or depressed. It is far more healthy to move through and release.

Once you have moved through the pain, you can then ignite the spark of creative energy. You can explore what it is that you truly want. Some of life's greatest hurts can become the impetus for your life's greatest gifts.

Chapter 14

Self-Deprecation

The programming that is woven into our daily lives is often reinforced by our own unconscious conditioning. Yes, you are consistently self-sabotaging the well-meaning efforts of your Higher consciousness. Every time you say something negative about yourself, you are deepening the conditioning of your past. Have you ever called yourself stupid, fat, lazy, ugly, crazy, weird or any other form of criticism? I am pretty sure 99.9 percent of the people reading this can say yes.

The key is not to live our lives thinking we have nothing to learn or change, but it is to recognize when we are putting ourselves down and to reframe what it is that we need to learn to work on. There is freedom in knowing that we are perfect in every way despite the fact that we all have characteristics, traits and idiosyncrasies that make us different from everyone else. This is normal and exactly the way it should be. We are MEANT to be different from absolutely everyone else on this planet. This is why we all have different fingerprints, cellular structures, tones of voice, handwriting, and the list goes on and on.

For instance, have you ever said, "I am fat"? I am sure many of you have (myself included). Let's look at this. Are YOU fat, or is your physical manifestation carrying unhealthy excess weight that it would benefit from releasing? You see the "I am" that is your true nature is not a physical material manifestation. Our true essence is our non-physical soul. YOU are not your body. When you can see this, your Higher conscious mind can search out the resources needed to assist your body in attaining a healthy optimal weight for your stature and body type. It may mean looking for alternative healthy foods that you would enjoy eating in comparison to the foods that you may normally bring home from the grocery store. It may mean finding an exercise class or video that resonates with you. I would not suggest trying a class that you have no interest in or eating foods that you detest. This is setting yourself up for failure.

I would tell you to look around for something of interest. Not only in exercise, but in food as well. Make a list of the foods you typically eat and look for healthier alternatives that are similar that you won't be disgusted by. I have found that if I am trying to eat food just because it is healthy and I don't like it, I won't continue to eat it. So, I have trained myself to look for what I like to eat, but in a more nutritious version. This way, you are not totally depriving your-

Self-Deprecation

self and you make small strides in self-improvement. Also, be open to trying new things. It is said that you must try a food seventeen times to know if you actually truly like it or not. Imagine that! Seventeen times. I have found this to be helpful. If I find a food I would like to become accustomed to, I will attempt to eat it numerous times before I decide it is not something I want to continue to try to enjoy. One food I have tried so many times and just can't acclimate taste buds to is most seafoods. So I don't stress over it. I know I have given it a solid effort and it really just doesn't appeal to me. So I have many other healthy choices I go to instead. Tofu was a food that I thought I would not enjoy, however, I gave it a shot and found that there are many ways to prepare it that are actually delicious. I crumble a serving of tofu in a bowl, add some pineapple and cinnamon and a little allulose and warm it for thirty seconds in the microwave and I feel like I am having dessert for breakfast. You just never know.

This comes to another point, give yourself permission to go at your own pace. You don't have to get it all done today. Small regular changes build up over time and are more likely to remain in place if you are not stressing yourself out over it.

You might also want to consider the use of the word CAN'T in your vocabulary. More often than not, when we say we can't do something in our lives, it is truly not a matter of can't, but of WON'T.

I have people tell me they can't meditate. I would challenge you to use the word won't instead.

Everyone is capable of meditating. The real truth is you won't put in the time or effort to sit in silence. It is too uncomfortable for you, so you won't do it. If you truly made the time to sit and practice every day, you would eventually get to the point where you are meditating consistently. A runner doesn't show up for a race for the first time and expect to win. It takes years of practice and consistent effort to get to a mastery level. The same is true for meditation.

I would say the most common apprehension to meditation is the misnomer that you have to sit for hours on end, completely clear your mind and sit cross legged on the floor. If this is your idea of meditation, I have awesome news for you!!! This is utter bunk! You can start so small, and make progress along the way. Start with just a minute or two. The key is to do it consistently, and work your way up. And don't worry about thoughts, they will come no matter how hard you try not to think. The key here is to notice when you have had a thought. You say to yourself "Oh, there's a thought" and then breathe in and breathe out and let it go, until the next one, then rinse and repeat. You will find after time, you will have longer periods of stillness. This is where the magic happens. The most important thing is to give yourself grace when thoughts arise. They always will. It's COMPLETELY NORMAL!!!

I will tell you, my meditation practice is typically only about twenty minutes a day. Some days I meditate a few times a day, but always at least once. I have meditated for as long as an hour and as little

Self-Deprecation

as a minute. It is just a matter of doing it daily and honoring yourself for showing up and practicing.

I also hear people say they can't lose weight. For a select few, this may be true. If there is an underlying medical cause or the use of certain medications can impose weight gain, but for the majority, it is simply not true. It may be true that they crave unhealthy food or aren't willing to take the necessary time to develop the habit of regular exercise. Many people will try these things for a week or so and fall back into unhealthy habits and they say they can't do it. It truly is not that they can't, but that they won't put in the work required. This may be hard for some people to hear, but if you are completely honest with yourself, you know when you truly can't do something, or you are just not committed enough to following through with the necessary actions to elicit the desired outcome. If this is what is happening, that is OK, but please be honest with yourself, because deep inside your inner being knows when you are lying to yourself. This goes for anything at all in your life you are dealing with.

Sometimes there are things we can't do, and that is OK. You just have to know when you truly can't or if you just truly won't. It matters!

Chapter 15

Grace

Grace is another one of those concepts that I had always heard of, but never really understood. It wasn't until after my daughter passed that I was able to get a handle on the idea of grace. I struggled with my grief intensely, and as I mentioned previously, I sought professional help to guide me in my healing. My therapist helped me to realize that self-compassion is a part of grace and that allowing yourself to be less than perfect is perfectly OK.

My grief came in waves. I would feel overwhelmed by it some days and other days I managed. But on the days that I was overwhelmed I found myself mad at me, that I could not bring myself to heal. I felt that because I had a strong spiritual belief that life continues after death, and that my daughter is not gone, she was just no longer a physical being, I should be able to come to terms with her new incarnation. When I expressed this to my therapist, she reminded me over and over again to give myself compassion and grace.

The idea did not become readily apparent to me. It took lots of time and practice to forgive myself for being human.

Giving and receiving grace was not something that only had to do with the passing of my daughter. I realized that grace is also allowing myself and others to be less than perfect. To be kinder when mistakes are made and to offer love and support instead of anger and criticism. This is something that I have struggled with most of my life, and even though I am better at it now, I still find times when judgmental, ungraceful human nature rears its nasty head.

Sometimes, I find myself being impatient with others. If I notice that I have been short with someone, and have not given grace, I will apologize as soon as I can. It is important to have the humility to admit when you are wrong and do what you can to make it right. Sometimes, it is not possible, because the person you offended was not someone you will see again. In this case, you must have grace with yourself, accept the mistake you make and make a sincere effort to be kinder in the future. Sometimes your harsh words make people not want to accept your apology. If you provide it with sincerity, and it is not accepted, you must then have grace for yourself and let it go. You can only control your thoughts and actions. You cannot control whether someone will forgive you or not, no matter how badly you want to make things right. Sometimes you have to have the grace to move on and vow to continue to make progress.

Chapter 16

Fear

We all have fear. A healthy fear can be useful, such as the fear of being hit by an oncoming car will tell you to run across the road. Get out of the way. However, in today's world, we have fear at every turn. We have fear that people won't like us, fear that our social media post will be ignored, fear of lack, fear of ill health, fear of stress, and the list goes on and on.

Due to fear, many people stay in jobs they hate. They are afraid to even look for another job because they fear no one will hire them or that they will not have the qualifications for another position. Some people even stay in unhealthy relationships out of fear that they will not be able to attract someone else or they will not be able to make it on their own. Due to these fears, they live lives full of stress, anxiety and unhappiness. People are afraid to make a change because the discomfort of their present situation is more comfortable than fear of the unknown. Please believe me that when you allow yourself to embrace the unknown, opportunities will open up to you that you could not even have imagined. Allow yourself to get comfortable with the unknown.

Every new situation will bring an element of uncertainty and that will force you to grow. But, this is OK! This is the real gift of the human experience. The gift of expansion and growth. I am not saying that everything you will try will work out as you expect. As a matter of fact, many things you try will not. But, this should not keep you from exploring the opportunities that resonate with you. Every opportunity you open yourself up to provides another layer of experience, knowledge and expansion. So what if it doesn't work out? Try something different, then try again, and then try again. Never stop trying. Keep trying until you find something that fits. Eventually, you will try something that feels just right. Like slipping into a comfortable easy chair. But you can't get there if you don't go through all the other experiences. Also, by having gone through the trying experiences and the experiences that didn't fit, you have amassed untold skills that will make you better at the one that does fit.

Due to our fears, we fail to communicate with the people around us. We fail to tell people how we are feeling. We have fears that stem from the idea that expressing our feelings will make people mad at us or look down on us, or not like us. Due to our fear of communicating, we will often allow people

Fear

to mistreat us. We decide in our own minds that communicating our feelings will make the other person abandon us or be angry, so we choose to suffer in silence. It is far better to communicate your feelings, because you may be interpreting things so differently than others have intended. You will never know unless you open up. Be vulnerable. Your vulnerability is your strength. By sharing your feelings you may just open yourself up to an entirely new and wonderful relationship. You could also find an end to a relationship, and as hurtful and scary as this may sound, it is far better than living with the daily fear of not knowing.

We stifle our need to cry because society has made the natural release mechanism of crying something to be ashamed of. When we cry in front of someone, we feel the need to apologize. WHY? It is normal, healthy and empowering to cry. To allow yourself to be vulnerable is one of the ultimate displays of true strength. We have been erroneously led to believe it is a sign of weakness, but nothing could be further from the truth. Crying is an outward expression of an internal struggle. When we let go, it opens us up to the aid of those around us who care about our struggles. Seeking help without reservation opens you up to a whole world of possibilities.

I am here to tell you that opening up the lines of communication is the best way to develop strong, healthy relationships. It is important to choose your words with love and care. You want to open the lines of communication, to use your words constructively and not blame or criticize.

If you are having difficulty with a person, start by telling them you have some feelings you are trying to work through and ask them if they would be open to having a conversation. Someone who really cares for you is sure to be willing to hear what you have to say. If not, you may be in a situation you may have to distance yourself from.

It can be scary to start telling people how you feel, but the more you do, the better you will get at it. Fear is also one way the ego tries to keep us from making changes in our lives.

It is not until we face our fears that we are able to see them in a different light. One of my favorite songs is "Say" by John Mayer. The words of this song detail the true essence of what I feel when I am looking to just say something. My favorite line states "Even if your hands are shaking, and your faith is broken. Even as the eyes are closing, do it with a heart wide open." I have spent many agonizing hours mentally rehearsing a problem and how I would express it to the person I was having an issue with. Only to find that when I finally opened up to just say what I needed to, things moved toward a resolution. It doesn't mean that the resolution was always a happy one. However, it is far better than being stuck and miserable. Once you come to a resolution, you can decide where to go from there.

Chapter 17

Worry

Worrying is a useless mind activity. It doesn't have any physical impact on the world. You may think that you can't help but worry, however, this is a very common belief that can be overcome. I am not saying it is easy, I am saying it can be done with practice. You will need to be willing to put in the work to get better at it, but you can improve in this area, and it will have a great impact on how you show up in the world.

Having had so much past trauma in my life, I found that any situation that would arise that could have a consequential outcome, would send my mind reeling on the hamster wheel. I would play out every scenario in my head, envision all sorts of dire outcomes and deviations. What I have found though is that rarely did things turn out in any way shape or form of what I had envisioned. The Universe has it under control. We don't NEED to shape a thousand different outcomes in our heads. This is mental chatter and only serves to deplete our energy.

What I have found is that when these situations arise, if I take a step back, take some deep breaths and come into the present moment. I can tap into higher guidance and make far better decisions. Slowing down to allow a solution to manifest instead of trying to control, gives us the space and grace to let go and let the Universe guide us.

Chapter 18

Grief

Moving through grief is a profoundly personal experience, however, there are some elements of grief that must be experienced to be able to heal. When my daughter Jenna and her father transitioned to spirit form, she was only nineteen years old. I was as unprepared as anyone could be for experiencing such a tragedy. I physically felt as if someone had burned a hole in my heart with a blow torch. The fire burning and the ache in the center of my chest was so intense for so many months, I finally succumbed to the idea of seeking professional guidance. I think that because grief is so innately personal, it makes it all that much harder to accept help to work through it. I assure you though, if you are experiencing grief, it is one of the most spiritual and loving things you can do not only for yourself, but to honor your loved ones and come to terms with the new relationship you must now cultivate with their soul.

The first thing I learned is that to move through grief, you MUST fully feel it and experience it. The physical and emotional pain is so intense that most people want to cover it up, push it aside or to push it down. Many people turn to alcohol or drugs to cover up the pain, but if you do that you are putting a band aid over a festering infectious wound that will not heal. I won't tell you that feeling these emotions fully is not agonizing, but the sooner you allow yourself to go through the necessary process, the quicker you will return to a life that is meaningful and fulfilling. If you leave the band aid behind you will see that the open air will allow the wound to slowly and naturally heal.

I also learned that the relationship with our loved ones is not severed. They are still with you as much as they ever were, if not more so. The true nature of all beings is that of pure Love and connection. We are all made of energy and energy cannot be destroyed, it can only be transformed. When our loved ones cross the veil of the body to spirit form, they no longer are constrained by the confines of a physical body or a limited mind. You have the ability to connect with them on a much deeper level than when they were in physical form. To connect with them, you need only ask.

I recall one morning after Jenna passed, I was having a particularly emotional morning and I just spoke to her. I told her that I was having a hard time

Grief

and she needed to send me some signs that she was with me. Well, I can tell you that over the course of that day and the following day, she sent me a total of five unmistakable signs that totally floored me.

The first was the appearance of the shape of a heart in my morning coffee. I was so excited I took a picture of it and just said thank you. I felt the deep connection. I then went to sit in my normal spot to enjoy the coffee and the sign of love and the Angel numbers 555 appeared on the clock. While this could be a coincidence, it truly felt to me as another sign. After my coffee, I went for a walk. In the clouds above there appeared an unmistakable image of a Phoenix. This excited me so much, as I have a tattoo in the form of a Phoenix in memory of my daughter. Of course I took a picture of this as well. It felt so profound and connective.

The following day, I visited my friend's gift shop and a sign stood out to me as if it were yelling at me. It said "You Are My Sunshine," and when I pointed it out to my friend, a light in the shop flickered. She totally agreed Jenna was with us in spirit and was reaching out. The significance of this is that my daughter passed the day before my birthday. Prior to her passing she had ordered my gifts from Amazon. They had showed up in the afternoon on the day she passed. One of the gifts was a little wooden music box with a hand crank that plays the song "You Are My Sunshine." I used to sing this to my children often when they were little. It touched me so deeply, I was euphoric with connection.

If all this wasn't enough, later that day I was looking to put something in the Bible beside my bed for safekeeping and I found a handwritten note from my daughter that said "I love u mommy soooooooo much get better Love, Jenna." I cried tears of joy. I have no idea how that note got in the bible, and don't recall putting it there or when. Perhaps she had done it at some point in her life, but I'm not entirely sure. But what I do know, is that I was led to it at the time it was truly needed.

My point is that if you want the connection, you need only ask. Ask with sincere faith and be open to the message. You will be pleasantly surprised at the unique ways you are contacted.

Since my daughter's transition, I have had the opportunity to connect with many people who have had loved ones pass forward. I have had the honor of being able to help console others by sharing my experience, and each time I do, I feel even more connected to her.

On one occasion, I had the opportunity to visit a woman who had recently been widowed, to offer some financial help in her time of loss. In our time together, she expressed her deep sorrow, sharing that she hadn't dreamed of her husband since his passing, which troubled her. At that moment, I opened up about my own heartache after losing my daughter, and how, in my grief, I asked her to send me signs that she was still with me. I told her that to my comfort, I received numerous unmistakable signs that she was near, all I had to do was ask and believe that

Grief

she would show up for me. I gently encouraged her to ask her husband for a sign that he was still with her and I assured her that he would show up. A few weeks later, I received a thoughtful thank-you card in the mail. Along with her gratitude for the gift, she shared with me that she had finally dreamed of her husband—he had come to her to say good-bye, and she said, "So thank you for that." Her words were a reminder of how healing can come in ways we least expect.

Chapter 19

The Words You Use in Life Matter

The words we use in life have a profound impact on our experience. It is so important to use words in our daily lives that uplift and support rather than tear down and destroy. It is so important to use positive self-talk when speaking about ourselves and equally important to use positive language when speaking of others.

The words we use shape the way we experience the world and how others experience us. Language carries energy, and when we choose words that uplift and support, we not only elevate our own mindset, but we also create a more positive environment for those around us. Positive self-talk is especially powerful. The way we speak to ourselves becomes the narrative we believe. If we constantly criticize or diminish ourselves, we reinforce feelings of inadequacy.

But when we choose words of encouragement and compassion, we build self-confidence, resilience, and inner peace.

Equally important is the language we use when speaking about others. Words have the ability to either heal or harm, and what we say can leave a lasting impact. By consciously choosing words that reflect kindness, understanding, and support, we strengthen relationships and foster a sense of community. It's a reminder that the energy we put out into the world through our words has a ripple effect. When we speak with positivity and intention, we uplift not only ourselves but everyone we come into contact with.

1. **Positive Self-Talk**: Instead of saying, "I'm terrible at this," try, "I'm still learning, and every attempt gets me closer to my goal!" This shift transforms a moment of self-doubt into an opportunity for growth. It's like giving yourself a high-five instead of a facepalm!
2. **Encouraging Others**: When a friend is feeling down about a project, instead of saying, "I don't know how you'll fix this," you might say, "You've overcome challenges before; I can't wait to see how you tackle this one!" This simple change can light up their day and remind them of their strengths.

Empowered by the Storm

3. **Daily Affirmations**: Rather than thinking, "I can't handle this," you can say, "I've got the skills to figure this out!" It's like wearing a cape of confidence and stepping into your superhero self, ready to take on the day.
4. **Compliments**: Instead of saying, "Nice outfit," you could say, "You look like a million bucks today!" This adds a fun twist and makes your compliment memorable, making the other person feel truly appreciated.
5. **Gratitude**: When reflecting on your day, instead of "Today was just OK," try "Today was filled with little moments of joy!" This encourages you to focus on the positives, turning an ordinary day into a treasure hunt for happiness.
6. **Constructive Feedback**: If someone makes a mistake, rather than saying, "You messed up," try, "This is a great opportunity to learn something new!" This turns a potentially negative moment into a chance for growth and collaboration.
7. **Supportive Responses**: When a friend shares their dreams, instead of, "That sounds hard," you might say, "That sounds exciting! You've got this!" This gives them the boost they need to chase their goals with enthusiasm.

The Words You Use in Life Matter

By sprinkling positivity into our language, we not only brighten our own lives but also create a joyful ripple effect in the lives of those around us. It's like turning on a light switch in a dark room—suddenly, everything feels a bit brighter!

CHAPTER 20

The Inner Child(ren)

You may have heard that we all have an inner child. An inner part of our past that has been left to feel unworthy, maybe less than, maybe incompetent, maybe sad, lonely, or hurt. You may have heard it is important to connect with this inner child and reconcile with that child. To tell him/her they are worthy, loved and understood.

I believe we have many inner selves. Not just an inner child, but an inner adolescent, an inner teenager, young adult, etc. I feel that we have so many aspects of our pasts that have not been looked at with unconditional love and compassion. It is no wonder that we doubt ourselves so much.

I started to try to connect with my inner child. I pictured myself around five years old and connected with all she had been through, and how brave she was at such a young age. But as I was connecting with her, a child a little older came to my attention. She

The Inner Child(ren)

was about eleven. She had a whole different set of circumstances that she was going through at that time. She was helping her ailing grandmother, she was trying to grow and mature, but she was also afraid and acting out. I then caught a glimpse of my teenage self. Just after losing her grandmother, she was tossed into an unknown world, frightened and trying to act tough and independent. I spent some time with my younger selves, assuring them that they had in fact acted bravely and strong for what was going on in life at the time. Each one at the level they were at had done the best they could for the maturity level they had at the time. Each one making their mistakes, but all were to be commended for continuing to handle life the best way they knew how. I did this mental practice and gave each of them love and hugs. Assuring them of their great worth.

This was a very healing exercise. However, it occurred to me that we not only have inner children, but we also have all of our past inner selves contained within us like nesting dolls. Each stage and phase of life has its unique trials and challenges. We all need to commend every past self for continuing to press forward no matter what life has faced us with. Because if you are still alive, you have continued to try. Every day you get out of bed, you are trying. We may not always rise to our potential, but if we are breathing, we are trying, and damn it, that needs to be celebrated. You are amazing for continuing no matter what.

CHAPTER 21

Masculine and Feminine Energies

We all have divine masculine energies and divine feminine energies, and we also have lower masculine and lower feminine energies. It is how we utilize these energies in our daily lives that determine whether we will have a positive or a negative experience in an interaction or a situation.

Masculine and feminine energies are not about gender, but rather two fundamental forces that exist within all of us, like the yin and yang of the universe. Think of masculine energy as the "doing" energy—it's action-oriented, logical, goal-driven, and focused on problem-solving. It's like the engine of a car, powering forward with determination. When you're getting things done, making decisions, or tackling chal-

Masculine and Feminine Energies

lenges head-on, you're tapping into this masculine side.

Feminine energy, on the other hand, is more about "being"—it's intuitive, nurturing, creative, and connected to emotions. It's like the gentle flow of a river, receptive and adaptable, allowing things to unfold in their own time. When you're in a state of reflection, enjoying the present moment, or tapping into your creative side, you're in your feminine energy. Both energies are equally important, and balancing them brings harmony to our lives. It's like dancing with the universe—sometimes you lead, and sometimes you let the universe take the lead.

Divine masculine and feminine energies are the highest, most balanced versions of these forces, while lower masculine and feminine energies can show up as their unbalanced or shadow sides.

Divine masculine energy is all about strength, leadership, and purpose—but it's rooted in love and integrity. It's like a warrior who knows when to fight and when to protect, driven by wisdom and compassion. The divine masculine is focused, but it's also patient, honoring others' needs along the way. On the flip side, lower masculine energy can be overly controlling, aggressive, or rigid, always trying to dominate or fix things without considering the bigger picture. It's like trying to force puzzle pieces to fit where they don't belong.

Divine feminine energy is the nurturing, intuitive force of creation. It's receptive, flowing, and open to the mysteries of life, but with deep inner strength.

It embodies love, empathy, and the ability to inspire without pushing. Lower feminine energy, though, can become passive, overly dependent, or emotionally manipulative, caught up in insecurity or fear of not being enough. Instead of flowing like a river, it can become stagnant, clinging to what's comfortable instead of evolving.

When we embrace our divine masculine and feminine energies, they complement each other beautifully. But when we fall into the lower versions, we feel disconnected—from ourselves and from others. Finding balance between the two is the sweet spot!

CHAPTER 22

The Law of Attraction

The term "the law of attraction" has been so overused and misunderstood for so long. So many people think you can just spout an incantation or an affirmation over and over and manifest all your wishes and desires. I personally think the term we should be using is "the principle of energy attraction or magnetism." I think people would perhaps get a better sense of how using our thoughts and the energy it produces to draw into us the people and circumstances we need to move forward in our lives.

One thing you absolutely need to do is get specific with your intentions. You have to think of precisely what you are looking to have, or you are going to get whatever is easiest to show up in your life. For instance, if you start thinking you want to have a partner or a mate. You may get one to show up in your life, but is it really going to be the ONE? If you want that special someone you will spend the rest of your life with you have to think about what you truly want in a partner. You have to think of what personality they may have, how sensitive are they, do they like the same things as you. How will they treat you, and how will you treat them?

If you want more money in your life, you need to get specific about how much money you want in your life. Do you want a dollar? Do you want a thousand dollars? Do you want more? You can find a penny on the street and you have indeed attracted more money. Get clear on what you want.

We all live and experience the world according to our beliefs. We experience life from our own point of view. Whatever you believe to be true IS true for YOU. If you believe the world is kind and loving, you will see evidence of it all around you. Everywhere you look, you will see people being kind and doing kind things for you. Conversely, if you believe the world is harsh and cruel, that is the world you will see and experience.

It is good to know, though, that you are capable of changing your beliefs. As long as you are breathing, you have the capacity for change. It takes practice to look for the good, but the more you commit to seeking it out, the faster you will start to see evidence of it everywhere you look.

CHAPTER 23

Practice Being Less Reactive

In the current digital era, the dominant state is reactivity. We are being trained to instantly respond and react to every little ping or notification that hits our email, Facebook, Instagram, Whatsapp, TikTok, YouTube, ClubHouse, yadayadayadayada. The list of ways to be distracted is so numerous, it is hard to even fathom. It seems like every day there is a new form of social media vying for your attention. It's as if we're all trapped in a game of digital whack-a-mole, where each notification requires us to react, often at the expense of our peace of mind. While we feel that these things are keeping us more informed, what is ultimately happening is that we are more distracted than ever.

I've noticed this in my own life, too. The moment a text message arrives, there's an almost primal urge to respond immediately. While it can be helpful to stay connected, I've come to realize the importance of hitting the pause button before diving in. Taking a few deep breaths can help me step back and assess whether the message truly requires an immediate reply or if it can wait. More often than not, giving myself that moment of reflection leads to clearer communication and reduces the chances of my response being misinterpreted as hasty or defensive. It's about replacing that instinctive reactivity with a mindful approach, allowing myself the space to craft a thoughtful reply. By practicing this, I've found I not only feel more in control but also build stronger connections with others, as my responses come from a place of consideration rather than urgency. In this fast-paced world, cultivating patience and mindfulness can be our greatest allies in fostering deeper, more meaningful interactions.

Chapter 24

Helpful Practices

Breathing

It may sound simple, and maybe even silly, but your breath is the key to goodness in your life. You can live many days without food, or water, but you cannot last more than a few minutes without your breath.

Breath brings energy into each cell of our being. Think of your breath as a generator. The deeper and fuller your breath, the more energy is being created and stored in your cells. This is why doing the type of strenuous exercise that increases our breathing rate is so good for us. It is literally generating power within the body for storage and use later. It makes you feel good by not only producing energy, but it also produces feel-good chemicals within the body.

Most of us breathe far too shallowly on a daily basis, and the more stressful life becomes, we tend to shorten our breath even more. I am sure you can understand that the brain requires plenty of oxygen to function at its highest capacity. If you are feeling brain fog, I would encourage you to practice breathing deeper on a more consistent basis.

If you stop to notice your breath without changing it at all, I bet you would find that your in breath stops about midway in the chest and your out breath will be equally short.

Now if you would be intentional with your breath for a moment, and breathe deep and fill the lungs to capacity and exhale all the way out, you would find this breath is much more satisfying for the entire body.

When experiencing tumultuous situations it is helpful to use deep breaths to center yourself. This way you can become like the eye of the storm. The center of the hurricane is peaceful, however, everything going on outside the center is chaotic and destructive. We all have the ability to use our breath to settle our center to be able to look at what is going on around us and to seek a reasonable solution.

Breathwork is one of the most beneficial practices that we can employ. The effects of trauma are stored in the cells of the body and the practice of breathwork can help to release the trapped negative energy that is stored in the body. I have found numerous teachers on YouTube that are very good at teaching how to use the breath to improve the quality of your life. Wim Hof is the first teacher I found doing breathwork, but these breath practices

Helpful Practices

have been around for centuries. I suggest finding a teacher and style that resonates with you. There are numerous styles of breath work including, but not limited to: Holotropic breathwork, Rebirthing, Transformational Breathwork, Diaphragmatic breathing, Equal breathing, Alternate nostril breathing, Vivation, Box breathing, Pursed lip breathing, Wim Hof Method, Connected breaths, Deep breathing, Lion's Breath, Breath focus, Five-finger breathing, Pranayama breathwork, and Resonance breathing.

Gratitude

Gratitude is one of the greatest ways you can communicate with your higher self. When you express gratitude for all the good in your life, you are essentially telling your higher self you appreciate what you have been given. Think of how good you feel when you give a gift or do something nice for someone and they express heartfelt gratitude. How does that make you feel? Does it make you want to do more for this person because you know they appreciate it? Of course it does. If this person showed no appreciation, you would not feel compelled to help or give them thoughtful gifts in the future. Think of it like telling your higher self, "You are doing a good job. Keep on doing what you're doing. I really like what you are sending me, give me MORE." The higher self is listening. Imagine you said thank you to the chair you were sitting in as if it were a person, and it responded to you with joy that you appreciated it. You can do this with all the physical objects in your life. Say thank you to the refrigerator for keeping your food fresh and chilled. Say thank you to the car you are driving for taking you everywhere you want to go. Now pretend your car or refrigerator said a hearty *you're welcome* in return. How would that make you feel? (Other than a little strange these things were talking to you, haha.) You would feel happy and because every object is created from the same energy you are born out of. It knows your feelings of appreciation. The more we express gratitude for everything in our lives, big or small, the more we are given to appreciate. Because who doesn't want to give to those that are happy in receiving. Everything in the world feels your gratitude or lack of it.

I personally can see love in even the most mundane things. When I look at a mailbox, I think "Someone loves to get mail and wants to keep it safe." That is LOVE. I see flowers in peoples' yards and think "they love their yard enough to adorn it with beautiful flowers." That is LOVE. When you see a road sign with directions on it telling you where to go, believe it or not, that is love. Someone loved you enough to tell you how to get to where you want to go. Sure, they may not have been thinking that as they were putting up the sign, but ultimately there is love in that action. The more you train yourself to look, the more loving your world will become.

Practice in your everyday life. Challenge yourself to find love in the most simple acts. Look at the

Helpful Practices

cashier and wonder, how is she loving right now? She may be loving her family enough to sacrifice her time to make money to pay the bills. She may love earning extra money to buy a new car, she may love meeting people and enjoys her job. Or, she may not love the job, but she loves something else enough to be there. You get the idea. Give it a shot. See just how many ways you can see love in life. You will be surprised at how it improves your outlook of humanity. Say thank you freely, and randomly, throughout the day. Over time, you will be able to see the benefits.

If you can imagine every little, or big, thing in your life and say thank you for it, and imagine that object feeling the gratitude and feeling happy for that gratitude, you will understand that everything is Love. If you thank the cells in your body for what they do for you, your body will do more for you because it feels loved and appreciated. Even if you have a physical limitation, thank your body for whatever it is capable of doing. Even Stephen Hawking, the brilliant theoretical physicist and cosmologist who had lost all mobility over time due to ALS, was thankful that he could still use his eyes to communicate through a computer that was designed for him. I can only imagine how grateful he was for all the wonderful people around him who aided in his mobility. Until our last breath, we can be grateful for something.

Prior to my daughter passing to the afterlife, she had begun to create a vision board. It was only in the beginning stages and she only had three statements on it that she had collected out of magazines. One of these statements was "Every object has a story worth telling, worth finding." At the time I couldn't really fathom the deeper meaning behind this statement. As I have grown emotionally and spiritually, the meaning is now very clear to me. We must appreciate everything. All the things we consider to be good or favorable, and even the things that we view as unpleasant or disgusting. She also had pasted "We're doing this for a reason" and "Turning catastrophe into a strength." Her wise words left for me to savor and contemplate. There isn't a day that goes by that I don't miss her physical presence, but I can still be grateful she remains with me in her higher energy form and that she provided strength and comfort for me in my darkest moments. There is indeed ALWAYS something to be grateful for if you look deeply enough.

One of the most satisfying and helpful practices that I employ is a gratitude journal. Each morning I try to write at least five things I am grateful for. One of the first ones is always *I am grateful for a new day*. Beyond that, I try to consider the day before and the wonderful things that have happened to me, or for me, the things I was able to accomplish, or the things I am looking forward to. I think of all the amazing people in my life. The ones I know intimately, and the acquaintances that help along the way. It is wonderful to just appreciate the checkout person at the store who helped you in some way. It doesn't have to

Helpful Practices

be anything momentous or earth shattering, just a little something to appreciate.

Sometimes just appreciating the sight of the bees collecting nectar from a flower, or the birds communicating with one another. There is so much to be grateful for.

It is important to not just write about these things, but also to feel what it is that you are appreciating. Not only will I express what I am grateful for, but I will include why I am grateful for it. As I contemplate why it is, I am grateful for this thing, I envision it and I feel the sensation of the gratitude for it inside me.

One day, I was not feeling particularly creative, or contemplative, so I just started writing. I am grateful, I am grateful, I am grateful, and so on. I filled up half a page with I am grateful, and by the time I finished. I really was feeling grateful. Sometimes we don't have to have something specific in mind to be grateful for. Just being is enough.

Meditation

Mediation is the practice of returning to one's essence. To sit and release the hold of external stimuli and to come back to your true nature, which is peace, Love, and compassion. It is in the space of meditation that we can allow the outside world to be suspended in order to allow for clarity and guidance to enter into our awareness.

Empowered by the Storm

Sitting in meditation is simply returning to your true self. To who you were before you entered the physical world. Like being in the womb. Calm, quiet, with no outside disturbances. It is your natural state of being. It is your true essence. If you could imagine what it felt like floating in the safety of the womb. The absence of need or desire. Your nutrition supplied by the Infinite Source. No need to seek out sustenance or comfort. You were allowed to just be. This is the state we can return to in deep meditation.

The strong drive of the ego mind is the cause of distracting thoughts during meditation. Our ego is designed to provide us with a sense of separateness, so when we enter into the space of meditation, our ego is left feeling as if it is not doing its job. It will consistently try to bring you back to a place of individuality, to disrupt the peace of the space of oneness. It will do so by flooding the mind with numerous, various thoughts and mental distractions. Thoughts of what is to transpire throughout the day, thoughts of what are you going to have for breakfast, thoughts of politics, family, and on and on and on. It is trying to bring you back to the individual self. The good news is though, that with practice, you can reassure the ego mind that it is not lost if it allows you the time to sit in peace and stillness.

By continuing to practice on a daily basis, the ego will become accustomed to taking a break. It will eventually realize that just because you are not externally focused for a time, it will not cease to exist. The only way you can assure the ego that it will not be

Helpful Practices

lost if you take time to meditate, is to show it. Show it by leaving it for a time and then coming back. Just like when a parent starts leaving a child with a caregiver. Initially, the child will be upset. They will be scared because they are not sure of your return. But each time you return, they become more comfortable and eventually, it is not such a big deal when you leave the room.

This is why I tell people to start small when beginning a meditation practice. A minute or two in the beginning, then gradually increase to five minutes, ten minutes, twenty minutes or more depending on your comfort level. You start by taking a deep breath and just concentrate on the breathing in, and then the breathing out. Follow the breath for as long as you can, when you notice you have forgotten about your breathing and you are having various thoughts, just come back to focusing on the breath again.

Accept that thoughts will arise throughout your practice, and don't feel bad or get hung up on the fact that you were thinking. Just acknowledge you slipped into thought and refocus on the breath. The goal is not to never have a thought during meditation, the goal is to be able to be aware when you have slipped back into the ego mind and encourage it to return to rest.

I have been meditating for years now and I still have times when I get up from meditation and realize I spent a good portion of the time in thought. I just shrug it off and know that next time will be more still. It's called practice for a reason. Just like a pro-athlete never stops practicing for games, the more we practice meditation, the better we become.

And the good news is that the benefits of meditation reach far beyond just the meditation practice itself. Meditation isn't just about finding peace while you're sitting in stillness—it spills over into your daily life in amazing ways. One of the biggest benefits is how it helps you stay calm under pressure. You know those moments when everything feels chaotic? Meditation trains your mind to handle stress better, like a mental reset button that helps you respond, not react. It also boosts your focus, so you can tackle tasks with more clarity and less distraction. And let's not forget the boost in creativity and emotional resilience. Over time, you'll notice you feel more grounded, less anxious, and even more connected to the people around you. It's like planting seeds of calm in your practice that bloom throughout your day!

Meditation Signature

I suggest that at the end of your mediations you incorporate a signature mantra that speaks to the intention of your being. I will share mine with you, and you are free to use it or develop one of your own.

I hold my hands in prayer at my heart's center and express, "I am gratefully and graciously accepting all the love, joy, money, and abundance this universe has to offer. I accept it into my heart and into my life." From here I extend my hands forward, out, and then open as wide as I can. I pause for just a moment and say, "I share it generously with all those around me," then I return my hands to heart, prayer position, and say, "and I welcome it back many times over, in so many wonderful ways. I am truly grateful."

Tri-Phase Breath Meditation

I developed a method of mantra meditation that I think you will really like. It has three parts. Before you begin, I would like you to choose a mantra for your practice, make it brief and concise. You can make up one of your own, or choose one from the list:

Om

- Meaning: The sound of the universe, representing the essence of all creation. It is often chanted to align with cosmic vibrations.

So Hum

- Meaning: "I am that." This mantra emphasizes unity with the universe and is often used in breathing meditation.

Om Mani Padme Hum

- Meaning: "The jewel is in the lotus." This is a Tibetan mantra, invoking compassion and enlightenment.

Empowered by the Storm

Om Shanti Shanti Shanti

- Meaning: "Om, peace, peace, peace." This is a closing mantra, often chanted to invoke peace within oneself and the world.

Ek Onkar Sat Gur Prasad

- Meaning: "There is one universal creator whose name is truth. The Guru's grace is the means to realize this truth." This mantra emphasizes the oneness of God and the realization of truth through the Guru's grace and wisdom. It is often used in meditation for spiritual clarity and connection to the divine.

Om Shreem Namah

- Meaning: "I bow to the divine energy of abundance and prosperity." This mantra is often chanted to invite prosperity, both material and spiritual, and to honor the divine feminine energy that fosters growth and success.

Satchitananda

- Meaning: expresses the idea of the highest state of existence—where one realizes the true self as being (sat), awareness (chit),

Helpful Practices

and bliss (ananda). It describes the experience of spiritual enlightenment or the realization of oneness with the divine essence, where the soul experiences absolute peace and fulfillment.

For the sake of these instructions, I will use the Sanskrit mantra *Satchitananda* (Existence, Consciousness, Bliss). Once you get situated in your seat for meditation, I would like you first to take three deep breaths in and exhale fully out. Then, start by imagining breathing in only on the right side nostril, deep into the right side of the brain. As you are breathing in, I would like you to say mentally "Sat, Chit, Ananda." Then I would like you to breathe out on the left side of the brain and nostril, repeating the words mentally "Sat, Chit, Ananda." Then do it in reverse. Breathe in the left nostril and left side of the brain repeating the mantra mentally and then breathe it out the right side of the brain and right nostril repeating the mantra again. Then I would like you to breathe in both nostrils and both sides of the brain at the same time repeating the mantra and then on the exhale out of both nostrils, repeat it again. Then you will repeat the cycle over and over again. You decide on the amount of time you would like to spend in this meditation. You choose the mantra. It could be anything you like. It could be as simple as "I feel well today" or "My life is abundant." Pick something that resonates with you.

Exercise

Exercise is one of the most wonderful ways you can create vibrant energy within your body. In my early twenties, my son's pediatrician made me aware that my smoking habit was causing my son to have a chronic cough due to secondhand smoke. Boy, did I feel embarrassed, ashamed, and guilty for causing him to be sick. I did not want my bad habit to be the reason for my son to be ill, so I was determined to stop smoking. First thing I did was tell everyone in my life who smoked, they could no longer smoke in my house. Even at this young age, I knew instinctively that if I were going to quit the habit of smoking, I would have to replace it with a better habit. So, the day I quit smoking, I started an exercise program, and I haven't looked back since.

Exercise generates stores of energy within us. It seems counterintuitive to expend energy to generate energy, but that is how the body works. The increased demand for energy for exercise tells the body it needs to produce more to keep up.

Exercise is a mood regulator, a health maintenance tool, and an energy booster all in one. What's not to love??? I know it can seem daunting, the thought of hours in the gym, but I can relieve that worry. It does not take hours. You can work out for as little as eight to ten minutes and feel the effects. I often do an eight-minute workout when I am pressed for time. I feel that a few minutes of exercise it way better than no exercise.

Helpful Practices

I am a big fan of exercise DVDs, and YouTube videos. I am always searching for ten to twenty minute routines that really feel like fun to me. There are several instructors that really speak to me. I usually never work out for more than twenty minutes at a time. However, this does not include my daily walk. I love to get out in nature every day, so that adds another twenty to thirty minutes to my exercise total. However, my daily walks hardly feel like exercise. I feel so joyful and peaceful when walking outdoors. I love to take in all the smells, sounds, and sights of the woods around me, or wherever I happen to be walking.

The point is, exercise is important, but it doesn't have to be a big, long, arduous task, unless you want it to be. Just get moving, and it doesn't even have to be a formal program. Yard work counts.

Ask Yourself Important Questions

There is a practice that I find very helpful when I am feeling less than optimal. If I am angry or frustrated, full of fear, resentment or lack clarity, I ask myself a question. The question is "What would it feel like to let go of all the anger, frustration, fear, worry or whatever else is spinning around in your mind?" Then, just listen to your heart for the answer. It has been my experience that a sense of calm and freedom settles into my entire body. I imagine myself actually releasing whatever it is that is plaguing my thoughts. I sense what it feels like to let go, to be free, to have compassion for myself. This practice reminds me of a Buddhist teaching: "If the problem can be solved, why worry? If the problem cannot be solved, worrying will do you no good."

But don't stop here. There are so many important questions you can ask yourself:

What would it feel like to consistently be in the present moment?

Why is life so miraculous?

What kind of person can I become that will leave a positive impact on the world?

Why am I so fortunate?

These are just a few examples of the types of questions that can generate a profound sense of presence and well-being. Simply ask the question and focus on the feeling. The feeling is the vibrational energy we emit into the Universe. The feelings we emit bring to us the energy of the world around us that matches it. This is the law of attraction. The more we practice emitting feelings that are positively energetically charged, the better we feel inside and the more outside positive energy is attracted to us.

Asking the questions forces our minds to think, and we can either think of negative things, which make us feel bad and emit dark energy, or we can think positive things that make us feel good and emit light energy. I don't know about you, but I prefer feeling light and happy myself.

Conclusion

I sincerely hope that by reading this work, you have gained some insight into the states of oneness and higher consciousness. I don't proclaim to know it all, and anything you read in this book is my understanding of these concepts. I have laid them out from my perspective so that you may benefit from some of the concepts that make sense to me. Please also keep in mind that any work ever written is a perception of that person's belief and point of view. You can choose to either accept or reject it. The choice is yours.

By choosing to employ the practices that promote positive energy, you set yourself up for success. And when your life is going less than you had perfectly imagined, the positive practices will uplift you and support you. By doing so, you have already won and indeed are creating your own reality.

Made in the USA
Middletown, DE
25 February 2025